Lily Samii

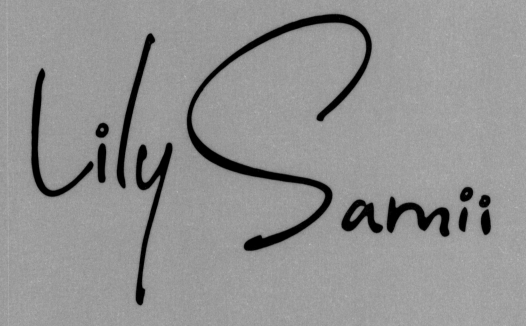

Lily Samii

A JOURNEY THROUGH LIFE & FASHION

By Teresa Rodriguez

Lucia | Marquand, Seattle

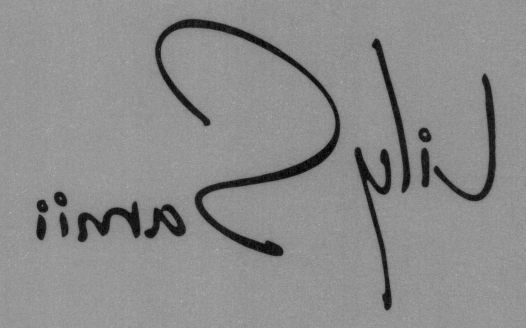

Lily Samii

A JOURNEY THROUGH LIFE & FASHION

By Teresa Rodriguez

Lucia|Marquand, Seattle

I am dedicating this book to my friend and colleague Kate Horan.

Kate's smile brightened the darkest corners, her elegance and grace were two of her favorite accessories.

She brought to this world an appreciation for beauty and a recognition of the finer things in life.

Although I can no longer hear her footsteps through the halls, I have felt her encouragement while making this book.

Throughout all the years we worked together, her goal was to help me document my life story and my work.

Well, my dear Kate, here it is! I hope you like it.

—Lily Samii

Kate Horan
April 17, 1964 - October 29, 2010

Library of Congress Control Number: 2020936582
ISBN 978-1-64657-003-4

Published and produced by Lucia | Marquand, Seattle
www.luciamarquand.com

Edited by Melissa Duffes
Designed by Aran Baker and Jenni Sandsmark
Typeset in Nobel and Bodoni by Maggie Lee
Proofread by Barbara Bowen
Image scanning by Gawain Weaver Art Conservation (www.gawainweaver.com)
Color management by iocolor, Seattle
Printed and bound in China by Artron Art Group

CONTENTS

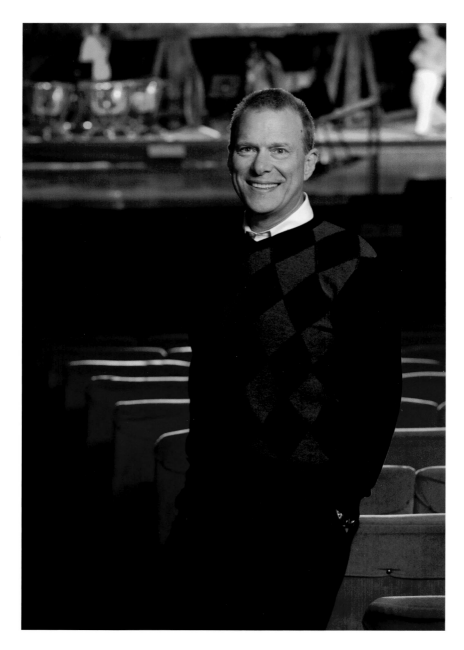

David Gockley at the San Francisco Opera House

FOREWORD

It is an honor for me to write this foreword to Lily's life story. I have spent forty-five years managing opera companies. The last decade of my career took place in San Francisco where I was privileged to direct one of the world's great opera companies, the San Francisco Opera. In addition to the lavish costume designs that these productions often require, the opera also provides the opera-loving community with opportunities to express themselves at premiers, galas, or even a simple cocktail party. It was in this setting I had the opportunity of meeting Lily. She has been the favorite designer to many of San Francisco's Opera, Symphony, and Ballet patrons.

Over the past fourteen years, I have learned that Lily's life is one that has included heroic rebounding from tragedy, injury, and upheaval—from her unlikely rise to one of the great couture designers of her time, despite not being centered in Paris or New York, to a quiet life in Marin County, a sleepy suburban area to the north of San Francisco's Golden Gate Bridge

A prominent theme in Lily's life—and in this book—has been her loving family and devoted relationship with her sister, Laleh, who has successfully brought her managerial talents to Lily's various enterprises. But in the end, it was Lily's quiet drive and gritty determination to find a way to express her art despite a roller-coaster life blessed with joys and fraught with tragedies.

The rich tapestry of Lily's experiences is reflected in her exceptional talent, her attention to detail, her social grace, and deep compassion.

Several years ago, Lily made it known that she wanted her story to be told, to leave a record of her life and work which would survive far beyond her retirement, full of exquisite photos of her design drawings and their realization into actual fashions. This is Lily's story. It is the perfect documentation of her extraordinary life and career.

David Gockley
Emeritus Music Director of San Francisco Opera

ACKNOWLEDGMENTS

I have dressed thousands of women throughout the last five decades. They put their trust in me for their most important occasions, and they became my family and friends. They treated me with love and respect. I have been the recipient of their profound dedication and their devotion. I'm humbled, and I consider myself one lucky woman.

One of the hardest parts in creating this book was the selection of photos—a daunting job. We had a mountain of material to choose from, and every box we opened brought back memories. For me, not only was it difficult to select the images, it was also an emotional roller coaster. As we opened boxes, I laughed and I cried. It has been an amazing journey!

I have been truly blessed throughout my career with the most loving and dedicated coworkers. They supported me through thick and thin. When I was down, they lifted my spirits, and when I was up, they joined in my elation, and together we marched on.

My thanks to my publisher Lucia|Marquand and their team who were very patient as they guided me throughout this process.

My sincere thanks to my uncle, Mahmoud Homayounpour, and his son, Bijan Homayounpour, for providing me with a wealth of knowledge and history of my rich heritage. Without their help it would have been impossible to gather much needed information and material from my earlier years.

Also, my gratitude to my team here in San Francisco for their hard work and putting up with my hyper-fastidious nature. Their incredible support is what keeps me going every day.

And, of course, without the unconditional love of my guardian angel Laleh, none of this would have been possible. Her unwavering encouragement through the good times and the bad helped my dreams come to fruition. She took the burden of running the day-to-day business and kept it off my shoulders. I was always the dreamer, and Laleh, the practical one.

Lily Samii

SOME MIGHT CALL IT LUCK,

OTHERS SERENDIPITY,

BUT WHATEVER IT IS,

LILY HAS IT.

For the past fifty years, Lily has shared her shining light and passion with the world.

This is not just a tale of an Iranian nobility turned fashion icon. It is a moving story of love, loss, and the dreams that have fueled one of the most successful fashion careers in San Francisco.

SHINING LIGHT

Ashi and Ahmad's love grew, and it reached its peak when on the 30th month of Tir 1323 of the Persian calendar, Ashi gave birth to a baby girl who was named Lily. Lily, who was so lovely and beautiful, soon became the shining light and the morning star of the family.

—Mahmoud Homayounpour

From left to right: Lily's uncle, mother, grandfather (holding Lily), and father

THE EIGHT HEAVENS

To truly understand Lily Samii and her incredible career as a fashion designer, one must venture to her hometown of Isfahan, Iran. Born into a family of both nobility and passion, Lily was given the rare glimpse of perspective. Her mother was a daring young visionary who cast her spell upon everyone she met. Lily's father adored her mother, and together they created an idyllic home for Lily amongst the breathtaking, mosaic-covered edifices in the beautiful city of Isfahan.

The city of Lily's childhood is famous for its iconic Persian-Islamic architecture. It was on these picturesque boulevards and brightly covered bridges where Lily spent her childhood. She lived in close proximity to the Hasht Behesht palace. *Hašt-Behešt* means "The Eight Heavens" in Persian and it is a stunning, seventeenth-century pavilion decorated in a multitude of colors and textures. It is these intricate silhouettes and rich shades that inspired Lily's creativity and appreciation for shapes and colors at a very early age.

This book is a passionate expression of Lily and her incredible life's journey.

The Bridge of 33 Arches, Isfahan, Iran

A NOBLE LINEAGE

Both Lily's grandfathers were respected noblemen. Her mother's father was Prince Abdol-Ali Mirza Homayounpour, grandson of Crown Prince Fath Ali Shah of the Qajar Dynasty. The prince was an admired officer who was known for his kindness. He married Ms. Farkhondeh, who was the daughter of Karim Khan from Naeen, Iran. Lady Farkhondeh gave birth to ten children; the fourth child was a beautiful girl named Ashraf-ol-Molook, who became Lily's mother. (In Qajar royal families, the title Mirza was added to boys' names, and Molook would follow girls' names.)

I was raised in a family where love and respect were the core of our existence. I watched the way my mother adored my father and her mother adored and showered her husband with love and respect. Every morning my grandmother, Lady Farkhondeh, would pick a special jasmine flower, called Royal Jasmine, and carefully fold it into a silk handkerchief for my grandfather to carry in his pocket all day, to remind him of her love for him.

Lily's paternal grandfather, Abdol-Ali Khan Eskandari, was a financier, but he was best known for his gatherings with poets and musicians. He was the head of the Department of Treasury and Taxation in Isfahan. But once a week, he would put aside his rigid work schedule to surround himself with kindhearted souls who brought with them their music and poetic musings. He married Ms. Esmat Noorsadeghi, and they had only one child by the name of Ahmad Khan, who later became Lily's father.

My uncles shared their memories of my paternal grandfather with me. They told of the warm summer evenings, fragrant with roses and orange blossoms, where my grandfather would sit under the weeping willow tree with his friends on massive Persian rugs draped on risers in our backyard. There, while his friends would recite poetry and create music on their traditional Iranian instruments like dafs, kamanches, and santurs, the birds would sit on the hedges and join in the chorus with their melodies. This interaction with birds and humans singing in harmony would delight me as a baby, and I would giggle to no end. Together the men would eat treats and sip aromatic tea while the day rolled into night.

A LOVE STORY

Lily's parents had an inspiring love story that continued for over seventy years and crossed every time zone and ocean. In Iran during the early part of the century, marriages were arranged for young people by the elders in their families—but not when it came to Ashi and Ahmad. Ahmad, who was an only child, was a frequent visitor to Ashi's house. One of her six brothers was his best friend, and it was always a joyful time for Ahmad to be amongst all the family and excitement of a large home.

On one of these visits, Ashi could no longer bear to just look at him from a distance and finally got the courage and found the perfect moment to introduce herself. Little did she know that Ahmad felt the same way, and his frequent visits to her family's house were not just to see her brother but also to get glimpses of her.

Their hidden romance continued until Ahmad graduated from English high school a year later. He then joined the Military Academy in Tehran and was awarded the rank of Lieutenant. During this important time in his life, he was appointed Assistant Chief of the military high school in Isfahan. Ashi was elated that her handsome officer had chosen to come back home and ask for her hand in marriage.

Their love was one where time stood still, and from the moment they set eyes on each other, their lives were entwined. Three years after they confessed their love for each other, their union was gloriously celebrated by matrimony. Together Ashi and Ahmad built a strong and vibrant home where they welcomed the most precious gift of all—their beautiful daughter Lily.

Ahmad moved his young wife and daughter to Tehran to continue his education. He received his master's degree in English Literature and started his career with the National Iranian Oil Company, where he thrived as a top international executive until his retirement. Ashi and Ahmad transported their love and admiration for each other all the way to the end of their lives. And like a true love story, they died within a few months of each other.

A CHARMED LIFE

For the first fourteen years of Lily's life, she was an only child. It was a charmed existence filled with everything she could ever want. For all the opulence that was bestowed on her, Lily found happiness in the simplicities of life, much like her father, Ahmad. Her father adored her—she was the center of his world, and their time together was filled with joyful moments. He was a respected gentleman and great sportsman, and Lily and her father engaged in many activities together—tennis, swimming, and horseback riding (Ahmad was a decorated equestrian), as well as winter sports, such as skiing the Alborz Mountains.

Lily's mother, the consummate hostess, was always welcoming guests into their vast estate surrounded by lush gardens with a gleaming pool as the centerpiece. Their home was always in perfect order, with delicious meals that were carefully supervised by her mother, who was an excellent cook. Their home was filled with the aromas of jasmine rice, pomegranate molasses, aromatic herbs, and cardamom tea. Lily's family's standard for excellence was a core value that is easily visible to this day in her life.

Her childhood was one of beautiful contrasts. While her mother governed the home with her creative spirit, her father was a gentle, quiet man who was completely satisfied in his life. He had a calmness and simplicity that Lily adored.

When I was just a small child, my mother would take me with her to meet Madam Sophie her dressmaker at her atelier to be fitted for whatever beautiful outfit my mother was getting made. I was mesmerized by Madam Sophie and the way she carefully worked with a tape measure around her neck and pins in her mouth, carefully pinning my mother's dress. To my mother's horror, I would ask for scraps of fabric from Madam Sophie to take home. I found such joy in pretending that I was Madam Sophie! I would try and mimic her by putting a piece of string around my neck—because I didn't have a real tape measure. And one day, my mother almost died of shock when she found me with a bunch of "dirty pins" in my mouth, while I was pretending to alter a dress. My mother did all she could to dissuade me from becoming a dressmaker. She signed me up for ballet and other hobbies that the family approved of, but I always went back to my scraps of fabric and pins.

My paternal grandparents played an integral role in my life. My father was their only son, and I, their only grandchild. They couldn't bear to be away from me, so my father built an addition onto our property. They left their house in Isfahan and moved to Tehran once it was complete. I was always in their arms, and they were incredibly protective of me.

Lily's first day of kindergarten at Bersabeh, the first western kindergarten in Tehran, age five

THE LITTLE PRINCESS

As a custom in Iran at the time, celebrating birthdays with elaborate fêtes were not part of the norm. So, it was very unusual to have birthdays like the ones Lily's family hosted for the young princess.

One thing that Lily never liked was the spotlight. She was not one to ever want to be the center of attention, nor did she care for it when people focused on her too much. But in her always-festive home, Lily's birthdays were very extravagant affairs that everyone in her family and friends looked forward to . . . except Lily.

Lily was always dressed in beautifully tailored outfits that were designed especially for her, so from a young age, Lily was exposed to the world of couture. Lily's hair was always perfectly coiffed, and her mother was vigilant in making sure that her daughter was impeccably dressed.

At the end of the birthday festivities, when everyone left and the house lay in silence, Lily would disappear into her world of creation, with her dolls and her incredible imagination. It was this brilliant ability to disengage from all that was happening around her that gave Lily the exceptional ability to become the designer she is today.

Lily's fifth birthday celebration with her mother, father, and friends

THE SECRET CHADOR MAKER

"

When I was nine or ten years old, I convinced my nanny to let me make her a chador. A chador is a full-body-length semicircle of fabric that is open down the front and worn as a veil. At first, my nanny was reluctant, but she finally gave in to my unending requests. I didn't want my mother to find out so I asked my nanny to borrow a sewing machine and take it to her room. I took one of her older chadors, studied all the seams and dived right in with enthusiasm. The sewing machine that my nanny had borrowed was an antique Singer, and it was so hard for me to crank the handle by hand because I was not strong enough, but I was determined to finish the job. I was halfway into it when my grandmother walked in! She wasn't angry; however, I could tell that she was horrified! The only thing she said was, "There is not enough time to order replacement fabric," since the new chador was for Persian New Year, only a few weeks away. To this day, I remember the fabric. It was a beautiful cotton voile with pastel flowers. I begged my grandmother not to tell my mother; however, since my mother was way too smart for this charade, she knew the whole story by the end

of the day and asked my nanny to try it on for her. I wasn't too sure if my mother was pleased or disappointed, yet I do remember she discouraged me from ever doing that again. Little did she know that the word got around and I became "the secret chador maker" for that summer.

BUTTERFLIES
AND FISHES

"

When I was a child, my room opened onto a long terrace with French doors that led to our garden. My favorite thing was to get home from school and run into my room to set up my fabrics—my grandmother called it "my shop." The fabrics were from scraps that I had picked up from my mother's couturier as well as small yardage that I would receive as gifts. I would arrange the fabrics in order of color, creating a rainbow of hues and textures. Then I would go into the garden and find something that captured my attention—from a flower in our garden to the fishes in the pond or butterflies fluttering through the air. I would pull from my fabrics to mimic whatever I was focused on, and voilà! I had my color palette for my next project! On my twelfth birthday, I was finally given a sewing machine as a gift. My very own! From then on, there was always a tug of war between my mother—who wanted me to have clothes that were either made for me or store bought—and I, who would refuse to wear anything that wasn't made by me, except things that I couldn't make like sweaters or rain gear.

"

Sheikh Lotfollah Mosque, Isfahan, Iran

THE PILLARS OF EXCELLENCE

One of the most valuable gifts that Lily's parents bestowed on her was the standard of excellence. Even though Lily's childhood could be seen as one of privilege, her family was rooted in the timeless principles of dignity, charity, and hospitality. Along with the scent of flowering Poet's Jasmine, their home was filled with the air of humility. They were securely grounded by their sense of service—to others as well as to the family.

Lily's mother was an integral part of the community, and so many people relied on her. She was always available to listen to a problem and give advice. Thanks to Ashi's diligence, her daughter learned firsthand what it meant to serve. So along with becoming a fashion designer, Lily is also known for an impressive list of charitable acts and donations—all taught to her by the graceful acts of Ashi.

From an early age, Lily was fascinated by the art of creation. Given the priceless gift of a sense of self, she was encouraged to try new things and passionately dive into the art of creation—which she did on a daily basis—and still does. Her perspective of the world was larger than life. While some might see the edges of a leaf as something beautiful to behold, Lily was trying to figure out a way that she could replicate that with fabrics. Before she became a famous fashion designer, she seriously thought about becoming an architect. That proclivity is clearly seen in her designs, as each of her gowns are structurally built with beauty and function, surprises and style.

The influence of Persia—with its daring use of colors and dramatic lines—is creatively interpreted in Lily's designs. The fourteenth-century palaces in Iran are draped in mosaic tiles perfectly placed with such great precision. Just as her family created a colorful and precise mosaic of home life and service, Lily learned how to replicate this perfection in her creations. So while her mother taught her to find solutions in any situation, and her father gave her a steady, calm, and patient hand, the culture of Iran instilled in her the ability to use shapes, color, structure, and architecture in surprisingly beautiful ways.

CAREFREE SUMMERS

At her family's summer home in the rolling hills of the Alborz Mountains, Lily spent carefree days with her family and friends. There they would hike, pick fruit, and play in the cool streams. Every day Lily and her friends would walk to the village to buy fresh bread and cheese. Lily delighted in the simpler ways of summer.

All photos: Lily, age thirteen, on vacation with family and friends in Maryghoon, Iran

That summer I was influenced by American fashion—my very first pair of Levi's, jeans were the perfect attire to wear in the country, even though it was not something you would commonly see women wearing in Iran at the time. And my scarf was very much Elizabeth Taylor and Grace Kelly!

Left: Lily at the Caspian Sea, age 16

Top right: Lily in Maryghoon, Iran, age 13

Bottom right: Lily and her father at the Caspian Sea, age 14

Top: Lily with Laleh, age 2
Bottom Left: Lily with Laleh, age 3
Bottom Right: Lily with Laleh, age 4

THE GIFT OF LIFE

In the summer of 1958, Lily's world would be magically enhanced by the birth of her baby sister Laleh, which means tulip in Farsi (both sisters were named after flowers). Laleh rocked Lily's world in the most amazing way; she adored Laleh and did not let anybody near her because she wanted her sister all to herself.

Laleh was a feisty little baby, so different than Lily. While Lily was content to be alone, her sister always wanted to know what was going on and was very curious. Lily enjoyed the challenge and encouraged her sister's growth and curiosity.

Lily asked her parents to not raise Laleh as she was raised. "Promise me that you will let her be like other kids." Lily's parents responded, "You have our word." And most definitely, they kept their promise. And when Lily moved to the United States, she again asked her parents to promise they would let Laleh visit every summer, which they did.

In 1979, after graduating from college in Europe, Laleh moved to California. The immeasurable bond between sisters has continued throughout their lives. Lily has always been like a mother to Laleh, her best friend, and for the past forty years, her business partner.

The fact is, when they put Laleh in my arms I didn't want to let go. That bond has been carried throughout our lives and continues today.

THE SHOW BEGINS

When Lily was fourteen, she was accepted into a French design school in Tehran, which she attended in tandem with high school. Three years later, she earned her certificate of completion followed by her high school diploma.

By the time Lily turned sixteen, she was brilliant at manifesting her ideas. Her creations went beyond designing clothes. For her sixteenth birthday, she decided to stage a fashion show in the large backyard of her family's home. She had a clear vision of exactly what she wanted—but what she wanted didn't exist, so she created from raw materials. Lily envisioned dramatic lighting around the garden and the pool and built lanterns that floated on thin sticks of bamboo.

For the fashion show, she designed exquisite dresses that she had her cousins wear. Each was beautifully tailored to fit perfectly. The designs were Lily's creations and influenced by her love of French fashion. The fabrics she used were unique to each dress. Lily beautifully captured the personality of each of her cousins with their dresses. While one cousin's ivory dress was adorned with a huge black flower that Lily hand-sewed to perfection, another cousin wore a flamboyant design made from colorful silk. Designing dresses that capture the uniqueness of each person has become one of Lily's signatures.

Lily and her cousins before the fashion show

As for the dress Lily designed for herself, that masterpiece was a work of art. It was carefully made from hundreds of yards of delicate French lace trim that was only a half inch in width. She meticulously stitched together each layer by hand, taking months to complete it. To this day, Lily admits that her sixteenth birthday dress was one of the most difficult pieces of clothing that she ever designed and constructed.

At such an early age Lily was a brilliant designer with aspirations that surpassed her years. This was only the start to her success that would catapult her into an exciting world of fashion in years to come.

Lily at her sixteenth birthday party

THE JOURNEY

Lily and Laleh at the Mehrabad Airport in Tehran, August 1963

During the Golden Age in Iran, both women and men were encouraged to travel once they completed high school. So, as a graduation gift at seventeen, Lily was given an airline ticket around the world. Although she was excited about jet-setting across the globe, she was sad to leave her sister Laleh, as she'd spent the past four years caring for her. However, it was set that Lily would travel from Iran, through Asia, to Hawaii, and finally to Los Angeles.

Bangkok, Thailand, 1963

AROUND THE WORLD

For respected families in Iranian society, it was customary that when children came of age they were encouraged to travel overseas. Some went purely for enjoyment, while others made plans to study abroad. Lily decided that she wanted to do both.

When it was her turn to fly the nest, Lily joined her cousin, Dr. Hassan Kamshad, and his family to travel east from Iran. First, they ventured through Asia, including India, Thailand, Hong Kong, and Japan, where they enjoyed the diversity of food and culture. Days were spent visiting the ancient temples and historic sites, where Lily developed a deep fascination for patterns, textures, and colors. The final destination for Dr. Kamshad and his family was Los Angeles, where he had accepted a professorship in Middle Eastern Studies for a year at UCLA. For Lily, the goal was to continue her travels across the globe, where she envisioned continuing her formal studies in fashion somewhere in Europe.

However, she decided with the encouragement of her cousin to enroll in the foreign student program at UCLA for two semesters.

Above: Bangkok, Thailand, August 1963

Hawaii was so heavenly, seeing the Pacific Ocean—it was lush, the contrast of the greens and the blues of the water. I remember inhaling deeply and just taking it all in, it was so beautiful. That was my first impression of the United States.

Lily in Honolulu, Hawaii, September 1963

This page: Lily at UCLA, 1963

Opposite page, top: Lily and classmates at Fisherman's Wharf, San Francisco, 1964

Opposite page, bottom row: Lily and classmates at Berkeley, 1964

A MULTICULTURAL EXTRAVAGANZA

When she finally landed in California and began attending UCLA, Lily took pleasure in the many glorious aspects of new cultures, cuisine, and lifestyles that her new home afforded her. Lily was indeed raised in an international, modern family, but there were still glimpses of other nationalities that she wasn't exposed to growing up.

One of the joys of living in Los Angeles was the trips she would take with her friends. Part of their multicultural studies included expeditions to destinations such as San Francisco and Berkeley.

RETURN TO OPULENCE

After two action-packed semesters at UCLA, Lily returned home for a visit. There she was greeted with all the love and warmth of a beloved child. They were so excited to have her back home. However, Lily informed her family that instead of staying in Iran, she would be returning to California to finish her degree and carry on with her life.

When I arrived back in Los Angeles with the intention of staying, I traveled with two large suitcases of fabrics and shipped two other items that were so precious to me. One was the carpet that was always in my room as a child, and the other was the old Singer sewing machine with a crank handle that I used to make my nanny's infamous chador. The sewing machine was the first item in my life that I purchased with my allowance and hid from my family for all those years. After settling down in Los Angeles, I bought a fully automated Bernina sewing machine!

Upon my return to Iran, it didn't take more than a day before I went from being a plain California girl back into the lavish lifestyle I had left behind.

Above: Lily, age twenty, in Tehran

Opposite: Lily and her parents in Tehran, 1964

BRIGHT LIGHTS AND SHATTERED BONES

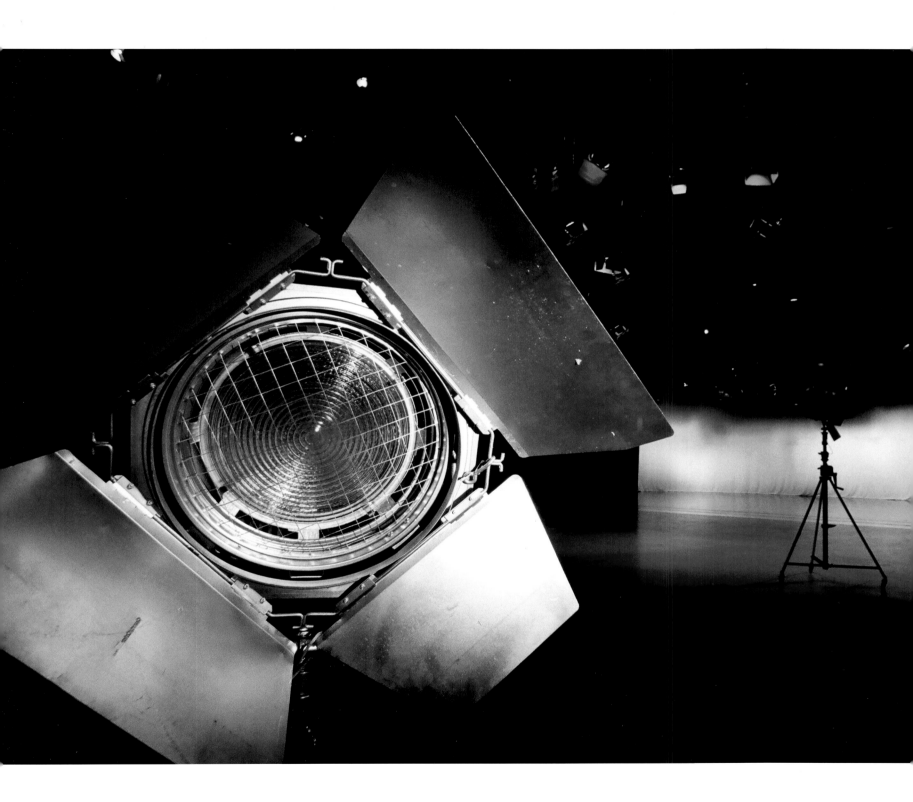

EDITH HEAD

Lily's career started when she was attending UCLA. She would pass a magnificent store in Beverly Hills every day on her way back from school and would often stand there and admire the beautiful gowns in the windows. Finally, a woman who worked there noticed Lily's fascination and offered her a job on the spot. The boutique was the only store in Beverly Hills that carried couture European designers such as Christian Dior, Balenciaga, and Chanel. Many of the social elite and celebrities of the time shopped there. Joan Blondell (the Meryl Streep of that era) was a frequent client.

I remember an experience I had working at the boutique in Beverly Hills that shaped my future. One day the store sold a Christian Dior gown, which had a white top and a black skirt, to a very famous actress. While the alteration lady was working on it, she burned a hole on the top of the gown. She went absolutely crazy—screaming, crying, and all that. I told her not to worry and asked, "Is there a fabric store nearby?" I ended up buying a yard of white duchess satin and copied the top in no time. In the middle of that drama, guess who came in? Joan Blondell, for a fitting, and she watched all of this unfold.

I was only nineteen when the Dior incident happened, but even at that age, Joan Blondell could see the talent hidden behind my decisiveness. Although the boutique was managed by women in their fifties who had been doing alterations on couture gowns for decades, I was already making a name for myself. When Joan would arrive at the boutique, she would steal me away and have me work on her gowns. As I shared with her my passion for costume design, Joan took me under her wing and introduced me to famed Hollywood designer Edith Head. I went on to assist Edith on three movies, The Cincinnati Kid, Marriage on the Rocks, *and* Ship of Fools.

When Joan Blondell was nominated for a Golden Globe award, she asked me to design her gown! Joan went on to win the award for Best Supporting Actress for The Cincinnati Kid *(1965).*

Making Joan Blondell's dress, I sewed nights on end. With the help of my little sewing machine, I sewed yards and yards of feathers all around her cape. I remember being overcome with emotion watching the awards ceremony from home on the television. When the reporters asked Joan Blondell who made the gown she was wearing, she said, "My little princess."

One memory I have from working with Edith Head happened during production of the film Ship of Fools. *She was fitting the actress Barbara Luna for a costume, and she had her hands under the garment around her bust area. "You have to go from inside and feel how it fits; the foundation has to be substantial," she'd say. "It can't move." That's what she taught me—the technique—so you don't have to keep lifting the strapless dress. To this day, that image occurs every time I fit a strapless gown.*

Edith Head always wore a mid-calf pencil skirt. She walked very fast and due to the limitation of her skirt style she could only take small steps. I could always determine which direction she was going because of her drum-like footsteps.

JAMES GALANOS

I was also very lucky to have the opportunity to intern with James Galanos. From him, I learned the importance of fit, finishing, and making women feel comfortable. He was a master at draping, and that is where my strength lies to this day. I was mesmerized by watching him drape the fabric on a mannequin and create the first pattern. Pockets were another important feature in his designs, as they put women at ease. This has stayed with me, and pockets have become a signature in my designs.

Another memory of James Galanos is the first time that I had gone to his atelier. He was sitting at a high table with his glasses on the low part of his nose, working on a piece of wool. I couldn't figure out what he was doing; I was fascinated. He probably felt my gaze, because he said, "Come over here—this is how you separate a double wool fabric." Using a sharp razor, he meticulously separated the wool.

James Galanos also had an impeccable way of finishing garments. He'd tell me, "The inside must be as beautiful as the outside." For the movies, the inside of the garment really doesn't matter. But for a client, it is very important. Throughout all these years, every garment I create is just as impeccably finished on the inside as on the outside, and all lined in pure silk.

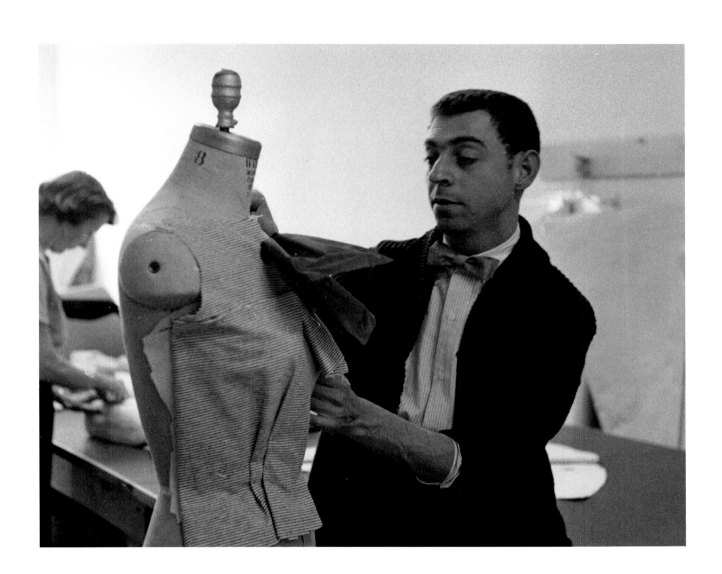

GETTING MARRIED

On one of her school trips to Berkeley, Lily reunited with her high school sweetheart from Tehran, and the passion that they had felt for each other so many years earlier rekindled immediately. They knew at that moment they would spend the rest of their lives together. This serendipitous reunion, which took place thousands of miles from their hometown, could only be summed up as divine intervention. Lily was filled with love and excitement for her new adventure with the only man she ever loved. It was a glorious time in her life. Lily's career was on a positive trajectory, and now she was reconnected with her soul mate. On one of her many trips to San Francisco to visit her boyfriend, they took a stroll to Fort Point. It was a crisp, star-filled evening, and under the Golden Gate Bridge they talked about how incredibly lucky they were to reconnect. That night, they made a promise to always be together, and became engaged.

Upon her return to Los Angeles and UCLA, Lily decided to take advantage of her school's holiday and go back to Iran to visit her family and also get permission to marry her sweetheart. With their parents' blessing, the young couple was married and returned to Los Angeles to build their life together.

Lily's arrival at her wedding.

After informing my parents of my intention to marry, they agreed, but out of respect for my grandmother and my fiancé's family, who were very traditional, my parents requested that we have the religious ceremony in Tehran and the civil ceremony back in California. It all sounded very doable and simple, and I thought we would go to the clergy's office and sign a marriage certificate. But I was so wrong! The next morning when I got up, there was a buzz around the house. Everyone was busy running around while my mother was frantically making phone calls. Come to find out, neither family was going to miss out on a full-blown wedding. My mother used all her charm and the top couturier of the time was called to make my wedding gown. The caterers were lined up and a wedding for five hundred esteemed guests took place in our garden in less than two weeks, because I had to go back to school.

Ironically, my wedding was the first time I didn't make my own outfit entirely by myself—but there was no way that I was not going to be a part of creating my own wedding gown! Of all the dresses that a woman will wear in her life, her wedding gown is the most important. I told the couturier what I wanted and then I would sneak out and bribe my family's driver to take me to the couturier's salon, where I would carefully hand-sew each of the delicate pearls and crystals to my beautiful silk Duchess wedding gown.

on her wedding day

TRAGEDY STRIKES

MAY 1967

It was 1967 and Lily's life in Hollywood was on a mighty course. Her experience working with Edith Head and James Galanos did not go unnoticed by other couture boutiques and designers.

Lily joined a prestigious team at a high-end bridal salon in Beverly Hills. It was a position she absolutely loved. Lily envisioned her life as one where she was creating costumes for Hollywood and designing the most amazing gowns for brides. It all was so perfect. But one afternoon in May, while she was working at the bridal salon, tragedy struck. On her way to a fitting, she missed a step on the staircase, tripped and tumbled down two flights of stairs.

The next thing I remember, I was in an ambulance—little did I know that the course of my life changed at that moment.

Lily's prognosis was grim. The injuries to her neck and back were extensive and she spent months in physical therapy. With a heavy heart, Lily's doctor informed her that because of the severity of her injuries, sewing was no longer a career option for her. The damage to her neck would not allow her to bend her head down for any length of time. Lily was devastated. Her whole life she found joy and comfort in sewing, and it was all taken away from her as her small body tumbled down two flights of stairs leaving her vertebrae shattered.

After months of rehab in Los Angeles, my husband and I moved to San Francisco to start a new life and be close to his parents. In the meantime, he was able to get a job in the language department at the College of Marin in Kentfield, a quiet suburb north of San Francisco. We rented a small apartment in the adjacent town of Larkspur.

Lily's body would never be the same, and her new life was filled with pain and limitations. But in the true spirit that is Lily Samii, she persevered and chose a new life path. She became an assistant teacher in the art department at the College of Marin. Her life went on in the sleepy suburb of Marin—nothing like her previous life in the high-energy, fast-paced world of Hollywood and Beverly Hills.

The only glimpse of happiness for me that summer was having Laleh, my baby sister, with me. She was only nine years old at the time and my parents sent her from Tehran to San Francisco all by herself! I'm sure my parents let her come see me because they knew it would bring me joy. They thought it would help me to forget about my mental and physical pain, and for the time she was with me, it worked.

Lily and her husband's apartment was walking distance from the College of Marin, so it was very easy for her to stroll to work. During her daily commutes, Lily would pass a nondescript store located in the parking lot of a gas station. She noticed very well-dressed ladies stepping out of expensive luxury cars in that dingy gas station parking lot and into the storefront. The only thing visible from the shop's dusty display window were a few bolts of cotton chintz.

I was puzzled; it did not make any sense to me. One day I finally went in and asked the proprietor of the store in a very curious tone, "What do you do here?" She, in response said, "My partner and I do alteration in the back." The word ALTERATION brought a smile on my face. A few days later I stopped in the shop again and said to the owner, "I have some afternoons off from my job at the college and I can sew, do you need help?" She looked at me and said, "How well can you sew and do alterations?" I thought to myself, "If she only knew about my years of experience and working with Hollywood greats!" But I said nothing.

The owners hired her part-time and told Lily that she needed to prove she was capable of doing difficult alterations as well as deal with clients who had high expectations.

Within the first week, Lily met a woman that changed her life in a profound way. Her name was Alice Zimmerman. In the summer of 1968, Alice was a frequent visitor to the alteration shop in the gas station parking lot. After a few visits, Alice started asking Lily questions about her background, puzzled by her incredible knowledge of designer clothes and sewing techniques. On one of Alice's visits,

she brought her daughter Nancy, an adorable and beautiful little girl. Lily guessed her age to be the same as Laleh and became so homesick that she finally broke down and told her story to Alice. Alice held Lily firmly in her arms and said, "You are not going to work in this dump."

Art and Alice welcomed me and my husband into their family. Thanks to Alice, now Laleh had a friend! Alice made sure that during summers when Laleh was with me, she would be included in all summer activities with Nancy. Both Laleh and I loved it.

It was a warm summer day in Marin when Art and Alice Zimmerman invited Lily's family to spend the day at their big, beautiful, ranch-style home in Kentfield. They were all in the backyard around the pool when the radio played a song with lyrics like, "I LIKE THE XYZ OF YOU." Alice, with her bright red hair and petite body, jumped from her lounge chair and said, "I got it, the name for our business." No one knew what she was talking about. But later that day while they were enjoying "Zim's" burgers (Art owned the famous Zim's Restaurant in the Bay Area), Alice convinced everyone that she and Lily were going into business together.

There was no room for discussion! Alice called our new business L.Y.Z, and for added clout, we added LTD. L and Y for the first and last letters in my name and Z for Zimmerman. And, this was the birth of L.Y.Z, LTD.

BIRTH OF L.Y.Z. LTD

Lily Samii, summer of 1969

L.Y.Z. LTD

Shortly after that glorious afternoon in the pool with the Zimmerman's, Alice came to Lily with her proposal. Together they would open a five hundred-square foot storefront in a strip mall on Magnolia Avenue in Larkspur, ironically, across the street from the gas station with the alteration shop. Lily did alterations at first, but it didn't take long before she started making custom-designed garments specifically for Alice and her friends. Unfortunately, the pain from her accident became overwhelming and Lily had to hire another seamstress to do the work. She hired Ann Pirenian, one of the owners of the alteration shop across the street. Ann was sweet and caring and worked for L.Y.Z. LTD for thirty years. Not only was she an excellent seamstress, she became Lily's surrogate mother.

To supplement the clothes Lily made, Alice took Lily to New York to shop for other clothes they could carry in L.Y.Z. LTD. They visited the Bill Blass and Geoffrey Beene showrooms and placed an order for a few pieces at each showroom. It was Lily's eagerness to learn all about the fashion and retail world that catapulted L.Y.Z. LTD into becoming one of the most recognizable specialty stores in the country. After Lily's first successful buying trip to New York, she was left to her own devices to follow through with merchandising. Although Lily's official partnership with Alice was short-lived, their friendship lasted to the day Alice passed.

Art and Alice Zimmerman, about 1990

On my subsequent trip to the showrooms in New York, I was terrified at first. I was in my early twenties and had to blend in with much older and far more sophisticated buyers from major department stores and boutiques. For the first few days, I just observed how the other buyers placed an order and the questions they asked until I learned the lingo of placing an order. And, most importantly, I studied how the female buyers were dressed. On my following buying trip, I was well prepared with my little black dress, strand of pearls, and sling-back, kitten heel shoes—not forgetting the red lips!

LYZ

DESIGNER COLLECTIONS

Larkspur, California

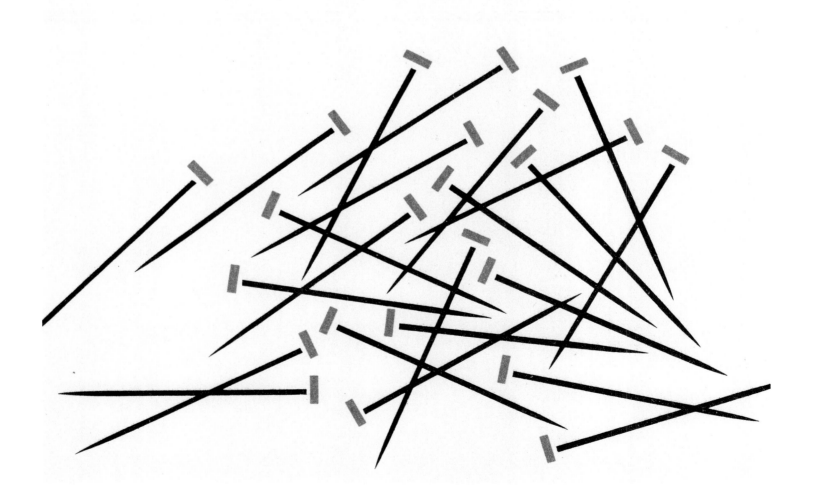

Barbara Boxer in her Washington, D.C., office wearing an outfit curated by Lily

"*I was running for local office in 1972. One day I was walking down the street in Larkspur and came across this little storefront that looked like a sandwich stop. I glanced in and to my surprise, it was a clothing shop. I am not a fashion plate and I never shopped in small boutiques, I only shopped at big department stores because my mom always said big store, you can return it, small stores, you can't return it. But when I looked into the window of L.Y.Z. LTD, I never had seen such beautiful clothes. I walked in and there was Lily. She was the sweetest and happiest person. At that time, I didn't have a big budget and I had to save up to buy her clothes. So, instead of getting two suits at a department store, I would get one suit from L.Y.Z. LTD. Lily's collection was so distinctive and sophisticated from what was being offered in mainstream department stores. We became fast friends and we would talk about our work. In 1982 I was elected to the House of Representatives. I told her that I was going to meet the president. She said she would make my dress. It was a bright emerald dress, with a beautiful wrap that I wore like a scarf. Ironically, I wore it recently—the piece is timeless. I have no idea how she created it!"*

—Barbara Boxer

REUNITED

In 1979, Laleh graduated from college in Europe with a degree in business and was ready to go back to Iran to start her career in hospitality and tourism. However, the recent news from Iran was very grim and a few days before Laleh's scheduled departure, the Iranian Revolution began.

At the time, Lily was in New York on a buying trip and decided to walk back to her hotel in the snow, deep in her thoughts about what was happening in Iran. There were two messages on her hotel voice mail—one from her husband in San Francisco and one from her mother in Iran. Lily immediately called her mother; her family was very concerned about Laleh returning to Iran. Lily agreed, and the decision was made for Laleh to join Lily in New York, and together they would travel back to San Francisco to wait for the outcome of the uprising.

Revolutions in Iran were not unexpected occurrences, and in previous attempts they did not last very long. With that expectation, Laleh agreed to spend a few extra months in California with Lily. After a while, however, it was evident that the political atmosphere in Iran was not going to change any time soon. Laleh then decided to stay and continue helping Lily with L.Y.Z. LTD.

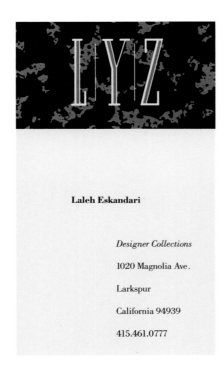

Laleh Eskandari

Designer Collections

1020 Magnolia Ave.

Larkspur

California 94939

415.461.0777

Opposite page, top: Laleh at L.Y.Z. LTD, Larkspur, CA

Opposite page, bottom left: Laleh and L.Y.Z. LTD staff member at a trunk show

Opposite page, bottom right: Laleh with L.Y.Z. LTD staff members at fashion show at the Fairmont Hotel, San Francisco

Left: Laleh's L.Y.Z. LTD business card

TRAGEDY STRIKES AGAIN

MARCH 1, 1980

On March first of 1980, my world crashed down again. I lost my young husband to a massive heart attack—life was dark. My husband and I were both at the height of our careers and still very young and in love. Our love never dimmed through the years and we looked forward to spending the rest of our lives together, but that never happened.

The only blessing was that I had Laleh, my sister, near me to take care of me. The roles were reversed—she looked after me and made sure that I was OK.

My parents moved to the Bay area toward the end of that year, and once again, the four of us were together.

I buried myself in my work and pushed myself to keep my mind busy.

THE L.Y.Z. LTD CULTURE

After the death of her husband, Lily put everything she had into L.Y.Z. LTD. She would spend long hours with her clients and worked hard to build the store's reputation. Her clients were now her family.

Lily's business life was running at a frenetic pace. She made appointments with the most prestigious fashion houses in New York and Europe. After a few years of carrying only known designers, Lily took risks with unknown labels. L.Y.Z. LTD was amongst the first specialty stores in California to carry Armani, Escada, Michael Kors, Oscar de la Renta, and other visionaries in the fashion industry. Once Lily was secure and had the confidence to venture out, she expanded her search for new designers.

On one memorable occasion, I was in Portofino on a holiday trip and noticed a beautiful store. I poked my head in and fell in love with the merchandise. I asked if they sold to anyone in United States they said, "Yes, we have a boutique at Bergdorf Goodman in New York." On my next trip to New York, I visited their boutique and said to myself, "I can sell this merchandise at L.Y.Z.!" The line was called Tiktiner. It was beautifully crafted merchandise made in France; however, the price points were very high.

Lily wasn't able to get the Tiktiner collection out of her head so on her next trip to Europe she made an appointment with them. She assumed there would be only two possibilities at this meeting.

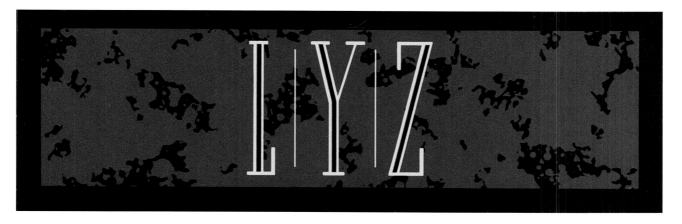

Either they will throw me out of their showroom, or they'll sell me the merchandise!

"

Until then, L.Y.Z. LTD was not getting much national press, but from that point on, L.Y.Z. LTD became the darling of the fashion industry and was featured in national magazines including *Harper's Bazaar*, *Vogue*, and *Women's Wear Daily*.

The truth was, Larkspur was very different from Beverly Hills, Hollywood, or New York's 5th Avenue. Marin was very quiet and laid-back; however, many well-heeled and cultured people lived in this tiny enclave of sophistication.

Lily was able to create an atmosphere that was very unique to the retail experience in any suburb at the time. L.Y.Z. LTD had an atmosphere of a social club, and Lily would frequently host events with champagne and high-end caterers. Her boutique was always filled with stunning flower arrangements, and she had a wine and coffee bar. Within a short time, L.Y.Z. LTD became a destination store, with clients from across the Bay Area and beyond.

The exterior of the store was completely different than the interior. It was like walking into a fairytale. As word got out about how magnificent Lily's boutique was, even fashion and merchandise icon Wilkes Bashford left the gilded halls of his opulent four-story palace in the heart of Union Square to drive the narrow side streets to get to Lily's shop and find out what all the fuss was about. When he entered her boutique, he knew at that moment that Lily deserved all the fanfare she was receiving. They became friends and professional confidants who would dine at Le Central often and connect in New York during fashion week. It was a friendship that has lasted through the decades.

All photos: L.Y.Z. LTD hosting a trunk show for New York Designer Stanley Platos

A NEW LOVE

Lily's chaotic life continued until 1984, when she met Mark Hormoz Samii. He was everything that she wanted in a partner and husband, and the bonus was that he had two wonderful sons. He was an elegant, charming, and gracious man, and Lily was enamored with him. He was passionate about life, and wanted to share his with Lily. He had come from a distinguished family; his father was a minister of foreign affairs and served as Iran's ambassador to European countries. His upbringing gave him the ability to learn various cultures and languages. Their love was one of admiration and deep respect for each other's life experiences. It was love at first sight, and they were married the following year. Lily wanted to spend time with her new husband, and she was tired of traveling so much for L.Y.Z. LTD. She didn't want to give up all that she had accomplished, yet there was a yearning in her heart that she wanted to go back to her love of creating.

While running a retail store, Lily dabbled in designing custom clothes for her special clients. By now, she had taken over the entire wing of that infamous strip mall.

WELCOME TO
THE MAIN STAGE

Fashion show benefitting Theta Delta Xi, March 1989

HARPER'S BAZAAR PRESENTS

In March of 1989, L.Y.Z. LTD partnered with *Harper's Bazaar* to produce a fashion show benefitting Theta Delta Xi, a very active philanthropic organization headquartered in San Francisco. The event was held at The Westin St. Francis hotel's Grand Ballroom. It was a sold-out show. In preparation, Lily scouted throughout her roster of European and American designers to showcase for the fashion show. In the late 80s, "slip" dresses and "grunge" was very popular, as was lots of beige. Color and opulence were lacking on the runway, so Lily decided to design and create a small collection filled with vibrant patterns and textures.

Lily walked into the Grand Ballroom the night before the event. The room had already been set up, tables beautifully decorated, and the runway illuminated with dramatic lighting. When she first saw the huge billboard behind the runway proclaiming BAZAAR PRESENTS L.Y.Z., Lily was so overwhelmed that she went numb.

After the show, Lily received many inquiries on the garments that were designed by her. Due to the popularity of her tiny collection, Lily hired two seamstress and dabbled in "manufacturing."

PRESENTS

September 1989

A Letter From The Publisher

Harper's BAZAAR is proud to present to you the exclusive boutique, LYZ, Ltd. This month, we join Lily Samii, owner and president of the company, in celebration of her 20th Anniversary of serving women of style and sophistication. The elegant LYZ boutique is located on Magnolia Avenue in the quiet town of Larkspur, California.

Since 1969, LYZ has been known for personalized attention, refined workmanship, and a unique atmosphere. LYZ provides affluent and fashion-conscious women with everything they need to create a total look for the season or for that special occasion. Lily offers her clientele the perfect selections, from breathtaking evening wear and cocktail dresses to unique jewelry, handbags, scarves and belts.

LYZ's trademark is Lily's special talent for giving each client a sense of individual style. Lily's experience in fashion designing and her appreciation of the art of fashion gives her the unique ability to create a complete look for a particular personality. Together, Lily's expertise in fashion and her incredible selection of designer labels and accessories have kept her clients returning year after year.

Each season, Lily travels to the fashion capitals of the world to bring her clientele the best of the American and International designers, Stanley Platos, Kevan Hall, Alfred Fiandaca, Mimmina, Tiktiner, Valentino, Mila Schon, Fabian Molina, Helyett by Basile, Paola Antonini's private line and much, much more.

Harper's BAZAAR is pleased to host this fabulous fashion event in support of Theta Delta Xi's contribution to the charities listed on the back of this brochure. We invite you to join us in the celebration of LYZ's 20th Anniversary.

Cordially,

Martin Schrader

Martin Schrader
V.P./Publisher

Alice Zimmerman had bought several tables at the fashion show to support Lily. During the grand finale, Lily walked the runway with her models, and the second she was off the stage, she hurried into Alice's arms. Their embrace was one filled with love and pride. Lily's place as a designer had been set in stone, and her career was about to take off like she never expected.

Alice was so happy to see me on that big stage. She was like a proud mama. It was touching to receive such a personal note from her after the fashion show.

Friday—
march 19th.

my dear Lily—
"you've come a long way baby!" your
talent and hard work has paid off and I
felt great pride in having picked a "winner."
The fashions were fabulous — the show
sensational and my friends and I "thank
you" for a delightful day.
Love—
Alice

LOVE
USA 29

Lily Samii of
"L & Z"
1020 magnolia avenue
Larkspur, Ca. # 94939

YEARNING FOR MORE

Mark and Lily spent a beautiful week in Lake Como to celebrate their anniversary. They toured some silk mills, visits that were arranged by one of her Italian vendors. At one point, when Lily was surrounded by the most luxurious and scrumptious silks, she knew it was her calling. That evening, as they were having a romantic dinner on the terrace of Villa d'Este, Lily was deep in her own thoughts. Her husband asked if everything was OK, and Lily opened up and told him the epic story of her childhood, and how she was yearning to go back to her first love—creating.

7th on sale

san francisco

**FASHION AND
FRIENDS
FIGHTING AIDS**

**SEPTEMBER 18,
19, AND 20, 1992**

7TH ON SALE

In 1992, I participated in the 7TH ON SALE event in San Francisco, which benefitted the AIDS Foundation. This event was very close to my heart, so I decided to take all the gowns that I had created for the show and donate the proceeds of the sale to the cause.

The event brought out all heavy hitters of the fashion world, such as Oscar de la Renta, Bill Blass, Carolina Herrera, and also from the entertainment world, including Richard Gere, Sharon Stone, and many others to San Francisco.

At first, Lily felt intimidated to be among such giants of the fashion industry. Nevertheless, like everything else in her life, she carefully observed the environment, asked questions, and before long had guests clamoring to speak with her about her gowns.

Shortly after the doors opened, Sharon Stone approached Lily's booth and proceeded to remove a red gown from one of Lily's display mannequins and put it on. As Sharon was mingling with guests while wearing Lily's gown, another guest, Rose Marie Bravo with I. Magnin & Co., inquired whose gown she was wearing. (Lily had known Rose Marie through their earlier retail connection in San Francisco.) Lily sheepishly said, "I have designed it." Rose Marie looked through the rest of the collection and mentioned that she was leaving I. Magnin to join Saks Fifth Avenue as president and chief merchandiser. She suggested that Lily put a small collection together and present it to the Saks couture buyer. Lily was stunned. To get that validation from someone like Rose Marie was beyond her imagination.

Earlier that year I had hired a young lady by the name of Elizabeth (Liz) Schumacher. Liz and her husband, Peter, had recently moved to the Bay Area from New York. Liz was with me at the 7TH ON SALE event, and on our way back we were going over what Rose Marie had suggested and drooling over the idea! I was not able to sleep all night, and the next morning we decided to give it a try. My professional life has been shaped by having people seeing something in me and encouraging me to bring my ideas to reality.

With serendipity as her muse, Lily had no idea what a treasure Liz and her incredible background would become. Unbeknownst to Lily, Liz's grandmother was Sophie Gimbel of Gimbel's Department Store, and Liz's father, Jay Harry Rossbach Jr., had been an executive at Saks Fifth Avenue for thirty-five years.

With Liz's encouragement, they put a small collection together and off they went to New York to show their first collection. They invited buyers from Saks Fifth Avenue and four other high-end specialty stores.

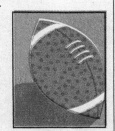
arks ejects nti-bias olicy

estern office's
-orientation
ng remains

By
ic Brazil
OF THE EXAMINER STAFF

a direct slap at its own West-
Region officials, the National
Service has refused to adopt a
y barring discrimination
on sexual orientation.

though the Park Service's
rancisco-based Western Re-
has adhered to a sexual non-
mination policy in hiring and
employee rela-
tions since 1988,
the agency is
balking at
adopting that
policy nation-
wide.

The decision
was announced
via memo by
Edward L. Da-
vis, the agency's
human-re-
es director. It seems to under-
he Bush administration's in-
ce, most recently voiced by
President Dan Quayle, that it
not discriminate on the basis
xual orientation.

n Henry, an attorney with
Western Region's Equal Op-
nity Office and a Park Ser-
employee since 1977, called
ecision "mean-spirited and ig-
t of reality."

vis said extending a policy of

7th HEAVEN FOR SHOPPERS

EXAMINER PHOTOS BY CRAIG LEE

Richard Gere *held a press conference and urged massive government support to fight AIDS.*

Celebs launch big AIDS fund-raiser

Star-studded crowd for 7th on Sale

By Mandy Behbehani
OF THE EXAMINER STAFF

San Francisco boosted the fight
against AIDS to a new level Friday
as the city kicked off its own version of the 7th on Sale clothing sale

Windfa spares big lay

$28 million from revenue refinancing, surplus funds eases budget crunch

By Jane Ganahl
OF THE EXAMINER STAFF

Once again, predictions of
gloom and doom for San Francisco's fiscal future proved premature,
as last-minute refinancing of reve-
nues and surplus funds gave The
City a windfall of $28 million and
spared hundreds of city workers
their jobs.

Mayor Jordan Friday released
his proposal for reducing The
City's $61 million deficit, and it
was mostly good news. To balance
the budget, Jordan introduced the
one-time $28 million windfall, ob-
tained from an increased percent-
age of San Francisco International
Airport concessions and the capture of surplus money from the
port and the Redevelopment Agency.

Jordan added to that a recent
Retirement Board overpayment of
$32 million, $2.9 million in late fees
for parking fines and higher Muni
Fast Pass fees, and $7.9 million in
"administrative cuts" in city de-
partments.

There would be, Jordan vowed
again, no new taxes.

VOGUE

The Condé Nast Publications Inc./San Francisco Office
50 Francisco Street, Suite 115, San Francisco, California 94133 (415) 955-8210

March 11, 1992

Lilli Samii
LYZ
1020 Magnolia Blvd.
Larkspur, CA 94939

Dear Lilli:

I was delighted to have met you last Friday. I can't tell you how impressed I was
with your business and your unique approach to retailing, the design world and your
location. It is always so refreshing to see an entrepreneur flourishing in these
difficult times. My hat is off to you!

I have spoken with Edward Menicheschi, VOGUE's Merchandising Director, who would
very much like to meet with you on your next trip to New York. He will go over our
various retail programs and how VOGUE can specially tailor an event to suit your
needs for LYZ.

You will also be receiving an invitation to VOGUE's Fall Fashion Seminar which
takes place April 14th through April 24th in New York. I hope you will be able to
attend.

Again, thank you for your time and I really enjoyed meeting you.

Best Regards,

Christine Mathews
Northwest Manager-VOGUE

CM:kh

*P.S. I have gotten so many
compliments on my
new pin!*

On our flight back from New York, Liz and I looked at each other, looked at the orders, and with horror in our eyes we realized that now we actually had to produce them!

Lily's decision to open a manufacturing business coincided with a dark time in the industry, when many of the San Francisco-based designers were closing up their companies. She decided to take the risk, however, and rented a space in the city and began to put a crew together. Lily needed patternmakers, cutters, and seamstresses.

One of her best decisions was to visit Celia Tajeda's studios south of Market Street, who was closing her business. Lily was so enamored with Celia, and together they kindled a beautiful friendship that has lasted throughout the decades. Celia went on to a very impressive career with William Sonoma, Pottery Barn, and Restoration Hardware. Not only was Lily able to hire a few of her people and purchase some pieces of equipment, but Lily also gained a lasting friendship.

Debra Kijawa, Essex House, New York, Fall Collection, 1994

ESSEX HOUSE
160 CENTRAL PARK SOUTH
NEW YORK

"

We set up at Essex House to show our collection. We had a corner suite with a magnificent view of Central Park, which welcomed the high and mighty buyers. We didn't spare any expenses; our suite was fully equipped with a butler, fancy food, and the best of spirits. Our account executive in New York was Larry Rotenberg, with a connection to every couture buyer that one could imagine. Our house model was the stunning Debra Kijawa. She was what the Lily Samii label was all about—style, beauty, and grace—Debra was my dream girl!

Larry Rotenberg, Essex House, New York

Debra Kijawa, Essex House, New York, Fall Collection, 1994

By Vince Maggiora/The Chronicle

Lily Samii at her boutique in Larkspur — she also has her own line of wearable designs for women

A Woman Knows What Others Wear

Frustration leads to her own line

BY TRISH DONNALLY
Chronicle Fashion Editor

Lily Samii has owned the LYZ boutique in Larkspur for 25 years. But a few years ago, she became frustrated when she could no longer find wearable clothes for her old-money clientele.

Prompted by her husband, Mark Samii, 63, she decided to try her hand at designing. Testing the waters last autumn, she introduced her first full-blown collection for spring. Samii's designs will be available in more than 50 stores across the country by fall.

After carrying such lofty labels as Giorgio Armani, Louis Feraud and Oscar de la Renta in her boutique over the years, almost 60 percent of the clothes in Samii's 750-square-foot shop are now under her own label.

"There's nothing really unusual about them, they're neat and comfortable outfits to wear," Samii says of the clothes she designs with the help of Mark Rex, 38, in her SoMa studio.

Simple Designs

Fine fabrics and impeccable workmanship set Samii's simple designs apart. Plackets conceal buttons down the fronts of blouses. Hems are piped before they're turned under. And every garment is lined in silk. (When's the last time you even found anything that was lined?)

"Lily Samii is a person who lives in the real world and designs for the real woman," says Vincent Knoll, vice president and director of couture and designer sportswear for Saks Fifth Avenue. "She takes figure problems for bodies that are not perfect and designs for them. She uses her own store like a laboratory."

"Clients walk in and there's total trust in me," says Samii. "I built up my (retail) business on that." She's using the same approach with her wholesale business, in which she shows store buyers how one blouse works with two or three outfits or one jacket works with a skirt or pants.

"I anticipated the first year would be $1 million and we're right on target," says Samii, a native of Iran who took French dressmaking lessons at the private girls academy she attended in Tehran.

As a newlywed in an arranged marriage, Samii and her first husband, now deceased, moved

Lily Samii's strapless bronze gown features tiers of pleated iridescent silk chiffon

to Brentwood. She took only two pieces of luggage — one filled with clothes, the other with fine fabrics. She studied fashion design as an exchange student at the University of California at Los Angeles and later moved to Marin.

At 11, she made her first bridal gown. At 18, she made Joan Blondell's gown for the Academy Awards when she won an Oscar for "Cincinnati Kid." Samii was working for Edith Head at the time. This spring, at 48, she made the wedding gown Nicole Boxer wore when she married the first lady's brother, Tony Rodham, in the White House Rose Garden.

The Fall Collection

Gorgeous pieces from her fall collection, which ranges from $600 for a silk blouse to $5,000 for a full length printed chiffon coat with clear sequins, include:

■ A mocha silk tuxedo jacket with charmeuse trim

■ A flowing silk georgette tunic with gold lace cuffs

■ A chocolate brown panne velvet gown with black lacquered dots and a boned cradle over the bust so it fits

■ A collarless jacket and matching tank top encrusted in brown and black tortoise shell sequins

■ A peach wool and cashmere chevron shawl collar suit with a flippy 24-inch long skirt.

The creme de la creme of the collection is a chocolate brown velvet kimono coat with pockets, $950. In the Bay Area, Samii's collection is available exclusively at her store, 1020 Magnolia Avenue in Larkspur.

Designer

From page D1

Samii's designs began to dominate sales in her Larkspur shop three years ago.

She had been invited to do a charity runway show for the Theta Delta Xi sorority in San Francisco, and "I needed some fill-in costumes." She created 18 dresses of her own, "and those 18 became the hot sellers of our store."

Two years ago, Samii was invited to join other designers in an AIDS charity benefit in San Francisco called "7th On Sale." "I met some people from the garment industry and major department stores in New York" who saw her designs and told her "you're crazy if you don't go wholesale."

She put together a "very small collection" in April 1993 and showed it "in an incredible penthouse with great models" to representatives from one major department store and five specialty stores.

All of them placed orders.

"I came back here and said, 'Oh my God, now what?'"

She realized it was time to "get serious."

She presented a second show in August, another in November. She has just returned from her fourth "extremely successful" showing of 50 more new designs.

"Now it's to the point where I've lost count. I don't know how many stores have ordered all over the country."

She shows her designs under the aegis of Essex House, a group of designers in New York.

The industry reaction to her clothes has been "amazing," she says.

When she placed an ad in Women's Wear Daily, "Everyone called. 'My God, finally something we can buy!'"

She has been written up in W and Vogue. In its August edition, Folio, the magazine of Saks Fifth Avenue, will give major attention to one of

SMASH ADS: Ads like these in Women's Wear Daily have boosted demand for Lily Samii's designs.

Lily Samii's store, LYZ, is located at 1020 Magnolia Ave., Larkspur; phone, 461-0777.

her designs.

Samii, an Iranian by birth (and by her sleek, dark-haired look), came to the United States as an exchange student majoring in fashion design at UCLA. Upon graduation, she went to work as a costume designer for Paramount Studios.

She followed her first husband from Southern California to Marin when he got a job at the College of Marin. She didn't mind the move: "I was too young and naive to be part of the Hollywood set." (Her first husband died in 1980; she remarried in 1984.)

At 49, Samii pinches herself. She is on a wild schedule, she says, keeping up with the escalating demands of her wholesale business and the ongoing demands of her Larkspur store.

But she wouldn't change anything. "This is my dream," she says. "It is happening right here."

Now available at:

LYZ

Larkspur, CA 415.461.0777

Superlative spring

Area events showcase season's new fashions

By Mary Apanasewicz
Fashion editor

Get ready to stash your rain gear and celebrate spring. From bell-bottom grunge to savvy suits to to-die-for-evening elegance, spring fashions are awash with color and making a big splash with luxurious fabrics.

So shake off the winter doldrums and rejuvenate the spirit by catching some of the latest and greatest outfits featured in these fashion shows:

■ **Social Service Auxiliary of Marin.** The "Spring Spectacular" fashion show and fund-raiser will begin at 10:30 a.m. Saturday with cocktails, a boutique, silent auction and raffle. Lunch will be served at 12:30 p.m., followed by the show that will feature cruise fashions (which complement the five-day cruise raffle prize) from Mondi, Cache, First Issue, Georgiou and jewelry from Imposter. Entertainment will be provided by the cast of the hit musical "Cole!"

Tickets for the event in the grand ballroom of the Embassy Suites hotel in San Rafael cost $35 and must be ordered by tomorrow. Proceeds will benefit Catholic Charities of Marin.

To make a reservation, contact Barbara Husak, 152 Dominican Drive, San Rafael 94901; 456-5569.

■ **San Francisco Symphony.** The symphony thrift shop Repeat Performance celebrates it's 20th anniversary of its fashion show and silent auction fund-raiser. Repeat Performance is at 2223 Fillmore St. in San Francisco; proceeds benefit the symphony. Tickets for the event, from 6:30 to 9:30 p.m. Thursday in the War Memorial Performing Arts Center's Green Room, are $25 and a quality donation of clothing, jewelry, furniture or other items. The show will feature fashions by such designers as Jean Paul Gaultier, Karl Lagerfeld and Nicole Miller. For more information, call the symphony's Volunteer Council at 552-8000.

■ **Junior League of San Francisco.** The 67th annual fashion show benefits several Bay Area charities, including Marin Child Abuse Council. The theme is "an excursion to international resorts of style" and will feature child and adult models from Marin and the rest of the

Bay Area.

The show, co-sponsored by Macy's and Lexus of Serramonte, will be held at the Fairmont Hotel in San Francisco on March 11 and 12.

Fashions will be provided by an array of designers, with a grand finale featuring ready-to-wear and couture collections from Pilar Rossi of Barcelona.

The luncheon shows on both days will begin at 10:30 a.m. with cocktails and a silent auction, followed by lunch at noon and the fashion show at 1:30 p.m. The dinner-dance on March 12 starts at 6 p.m.; the show is at 8:15 and the dinner at 9. Luncheon tickets are $75 and the dinner show is $140. Call 567-8600 for tickets and more information.

■ **Bettina.** This Mill Valley women's store will host a fashion and trunk show March 16 highlighting the spring/summer and the San Francisco Symphony's Black & White Ball evening wear collections from Russian designer Irenka Kantsova.

A champagne reception will be held from 5 to 9 p.m., with the showing at 6:30. Some designs will be available for purchase and orders will be taken. Kantsova is an award-winning designer from the Moscow area who now resides in the United States.

The shop, owned by sisters Doretta and Bettina Boehm, is located at 410 Strawberry Village. Admission is free. For more information, call 389-9418.

■ **LYZ.** Designer Lily Samii, who owns the Larkspur retail store, will show her spring collections at a runway show March 17 in the grand ballroom of the Fairmont Hotel in San Francisco.

The show, which will benefit the Bay Area philanthropic organization Theta Delta Xi, begins at 11:30 a.m. with no-host cocktails followed by lunch at 12:30 p.m. The show will start about 1:30.

Being fashionable around the world is the theme of the show, which will feature everything from tropical and nautical outfits to daywear to ball gowns. Tickets are $65. For more information, call LYZ at 461-0777.

■ **Vintage Fashion Expo.** More than 100 dealers from throughout the country will be selling clothing, jewelry and accessories from the 1850s through the 1950s, and covering eight centuries

and European style periods.

The expo will be held March 27 and 28 at the Concourse at 8th and Brannan streets in San Francisco.

Shopping hours will run from 10 a.m.

to 5 p.m. both days with daily fashion shows at 1:30 and lectures on vintage subjects at noon and 3 o'clock. Admission is $5. For more information, call 510-653-1087.

PLAYFUL ELEGANCE: The sequined top of this black, two-piece evening suit by Lily Samii, owner of LYZ in Larkspur, softly molds to the wearer's body. The lined pants are a luxurious pleated chiffon.

WEATHER: Scattered showers tonight and tomorrow; possible thunderstorms. Lows, 45. Highs, 75. Details, A2.

Home delivery 1-800-660-0760 35 cents

Marin Independent Journal

May 6, 1994

FRIDAY

● Marin County, California

Candidates

Home sales

in

36

CCESS
design

nii got her start here,
r label is a national hit

hley

res writer

ON DESIGNER Lily Samii
d her Larkspur shop LYZ
ars ago "in an unheard-of lo-
, with no capital." At times
night to meet customer

young. I went against every
' she says.

clothes are in Saks, Neiman
agnin, Nordstrom. Stores are
her designs.

ible," she says.

-hit Lily Samii label, fea-
en's Wear Daily, is being
-drawer fashion outlets
e country.

xer wore clothing from LYZ
ng-in as a U.S. senator and
terward. Later this month,
e senator's daughter, Nicole,
amii-designed wedding dress
first lady's brother, Tony
he Rose Garden of the

come a long way.

In 1969, Samii opened LYZ, an out-of-
the-way dress shop in a Larkspur mini
shopping center. She made a few outfits,
sold them, and used the profits to make
several more.

The shop prospered, thanks to a well-
heeled clientele that was looking for luxury fabrics and quality workmanship.

To keep up with customer demand, Samii began selling dresses by top-of-the-
line European designers, supplementing
them each season with a dozen outfits of
her own.

LYZ quickly attracted customers from
San Francisco, the Peninsula and the
East Bay as well as Marin, Sen. Boxer of
Greenbrae among them.

Samii says she probably would have
been content with her success had she not
become frustrated a few years ago by her
inability to find European clothes beautiful enough for her clientele.

Several of her overseas designers had
gone out of business; some had died of
AIDS. Among other designers, she says,
the grunge look was in; their fashions
were too extreme. "I could find nothing
that a real person would wear."

She came home from buying trips wor-
rying "What am I going to do for Mrs.
So-and-So?" who was relying on her for
clothes.

The solution, she finally recognized,
was a dress line of her own.

"She understands the customer because
of her retail background and she is exactly
what the retail customer is looking for,"
says Mary Jane Denzer, a new Samii customer who owns a designer boutique in
White Plains, N.Y.

Lily Samii went wholesale one year ago.
She now spends a hefty part of her sev-
en-day work week at her 5,000-square-foot
design studio on Second Street in San
Francisco, where 19 cutters, designers and
seamstresses prepare her designs. A number of seamstresses also work for her in
Marin.

Wholesale is the proper term for her
new venture, but her clothes are still indi-
vidually cut and hand sewn. The fabrics
are still imported, mostly from Italy. The
hand-made lace trim still comes from
Austria and France.

The dresses still cost from $800 to
$5,000 or $6,000.

She first established her reputation as a
designer of evening wear. Her designs
were simple, classic, elegant, to show off
the beauty of the fabrics.

Gradually she introduced day wear, and
today combines evening gowns with simple suits and special occasion dresses.

See Designer, page D3

ELEGANT BUT WEARABLE: This cocktail dress by Lily
Samii is made of wool crepe trimmed with satin. It has a flippy
skirt and beautifully detailed sleeves and can be worn with or
without a matching cape. Samii's prices are steep: $800 to
$5,000 or $6,000 per dress.

Lily Samii photo

Sen. Barbara Boxer's daughter,
Nicole, will wear a Samii-designed
dress to marry the first lady's
brother, Tony Rodham, in the
White House Rose Garden.

LILY SAMII: A
native of Iran, she
came to the United
States as an
exchange student
majoring in fashion
at UCLA. After
graduation, she
worked as a
costume designer
for Paramount. She
and her first
husband moved to
Marin when he got a
job at the College of
Marin.

Lily Samii

Larkspur designer is all the fashion

Next showing to be at
White House wedding

Lifestyles **D1**

NEW CFO AT DONNA KARAN/2   BDO SEIDMAN HITS BACK ON LESLIE FAY/2

Women's Wear Daily • The Retailers' Daily Newspaper • August 18, 1994 Vol. 168, No. 36 $1.25

WWDTHURSDAY

LILY'S LATEST LABEL

Lily Samii was happy just
being a retailer, carrying such
labels as Giorgio Armani, Escada and Louis Feraud at
LYZ, the Marin County boutique she launched 25 years
ago.

Then came grunge.

The street-influenced styles
of grunge shown by many top
designers weren't likely to play
to Samii's more traditional customer. "When we went into the
grunge period, my buying trips
were disasters," Samii says. "I
couldn't come up with anything. My budget to buy was un-
touched when I came back
from the trips."

Samii had to improvise.
Two years ago, preparing for a
charity fashion show to be
sponsored by her boutique in
Larkspur, she decided to supplement what little she ordered from New York and Europe with a few styles she designed herself. To her surprise, her own pieces proved
to be bestsellers.

Thus began Lily Samii, a line of
better-priced, special-occasion appar-
el that she now sells in LYZ as well as
to other specialty stores. Since

Lily Samii with
one of her designs.

launching the collection a year ago,
Samii has rung up $1 million in or-
ders from Saks Fifth Avenue, Neiman
Marcus and smaller specialty stores
such as Marissa in Naples, Fla., and

Mary Jane Benzer in
White Plains, N.Y.
About 60 percent of
the sales at LYZ are
generated from Lily
Samii. Wholesale
prices range from $250
for a silk blouse to
$2,500 for a panné vel-
vet gown. One of
Samii's design inspi-
rations is today's
mother of the bride.

"I was looking at
the mothers of the
bride who would
never be caught dead
in chiffons and bead-
ed stuff," Samii says.
"They look like their
daughters' sisters, not
their mothers. They
want to look smart."

Business has been
so strong that Samii
recently moved her
design studios from
her Magnolia Avenue
store in Larkspur to
San Francisco. The
new studio, located on
Second Street in the
South of Market dis-
trict, includes design,
sample-making and
some production facili-
ties.

"I had no idea this
would get so big so
fast," Samii admits.
"I'm really doing this
as a challenge, and I
like helping other re-
tailers. I know how
frustrated they have
been the past few sea-
sons."

**Lily Samii's black
beaded silk lace gown.**

PHOTOS BY TED DAYTON

ONWARDS AND UPWARDS

"Lily Samii is a person who lives in the real world and designs for the real woman," says Vincent Knoll, vice president and director of couture and designer sportswear for Saks Fifth Avenue. "She takes figure problems for bodies that are not perfect and designs for them. She uses her own store like a laboratory."

—*Trish Donnally*, San Francisco Chronicle, *Tuesday, June 21, 1994*

This beautiful tulle was my first pur-chase as a fashion designer at the Première Vision in Paris. I walked into Jacob Schlaepfer's showroom and fell in love with it, not knowing what I was going to do with it. I just had to have it. Years later when I was asked to participate at the Perrier-Jouët 100th anniversary of Belle Époque, I was asked to dress Mrs. Denise Hale of San Francisco to attend the event in Épernay, France. I asked Jacob Schlaepfer to reproduce the fabric for me since the flowers resembled the flowers on the Belle Époque bottle.

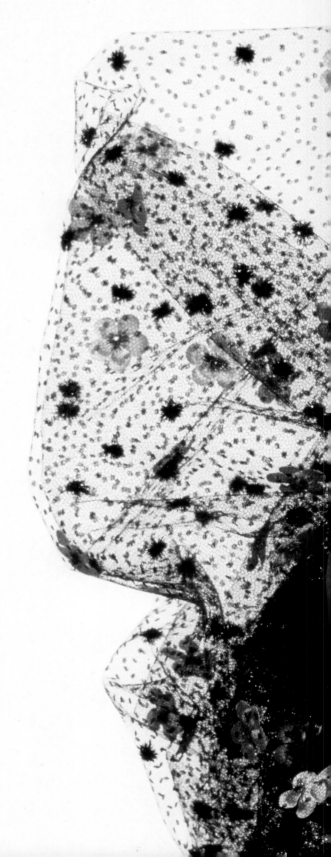

Lily Samii

Now available at:

LYZ

Larkspur, CA 415.461.0777

Marin Independent Journal • Thursday, September 3, 1998

LIFESTYLES

D

Pamela Moreland, Features Editor 382-7263

Fashioned for success

Lily Samii

An overnight success after 30 years — that's how Lily Samii describes herself, laughing in a charming, self-deprecating way as she gestures around the light-filled, elegant San Francisco showroom on Stockton Street that she opened on April 9. It's up on the third floor. There's no exterior sign. You could be in Paris. And that's a big plus for Samii clients, who want to relax in discreet, posh surroundings as they try on Samii's plush gowns.

Samii, who many Marin socialites view as one of our county's best-kept fashion secrets, has owned the LYZ boutique on Magnolia Avenue in Larkspur since the 1960s. Over time, her line of cocktail suits, frocks and gowns has expanded — and sold well enough, all through word of mouth — that Samii now has a showroom in Manhattan and recently purchased a 1920s building in downtown San Francisco where her 30 employees produce Lily Samii clothes and handbags.

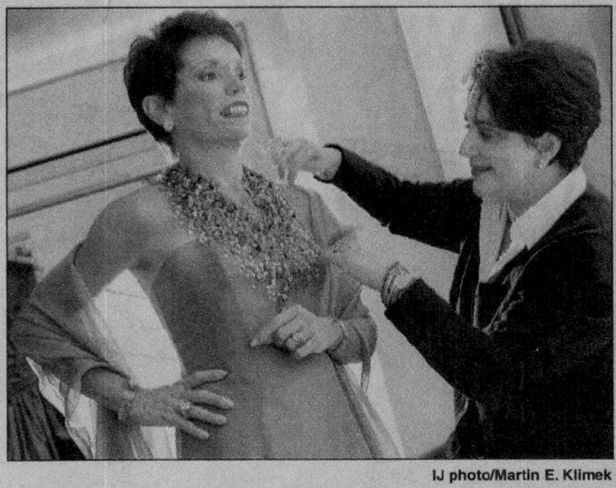

IJ photo/Martin E. Klimek

SAKS FIFTH AVENUE

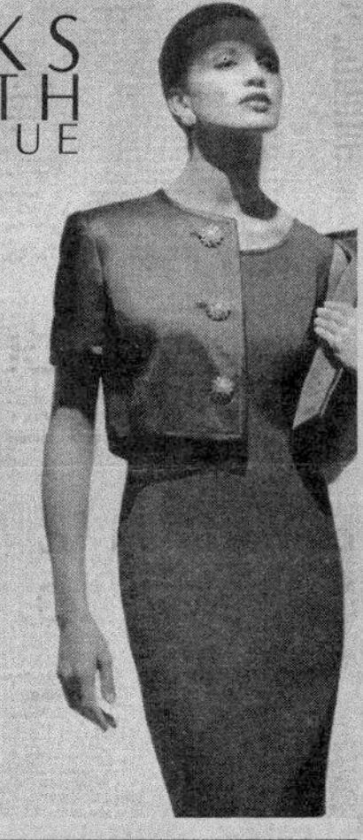

Contrasting textures by **Lily Samii.**

Jewel-button satin jacket over crepe dress. All in navy silk. Evening Salon on Three in New York and select SFA stores nationwide.

Grace's is pleased to welcome back one of America's most exciting new designers, Lily Samii. From San Francisco to Nashville she will introduce for Spring 1996 her concept of luxury separates for day and evening in fine fabrics with classic European styling. Exclusively at Grace's, Thursday and Friday, February 1 and 2 in our Green Hills Shop.

Grace's

Grace's Plaza
4005 Hillsboro Road

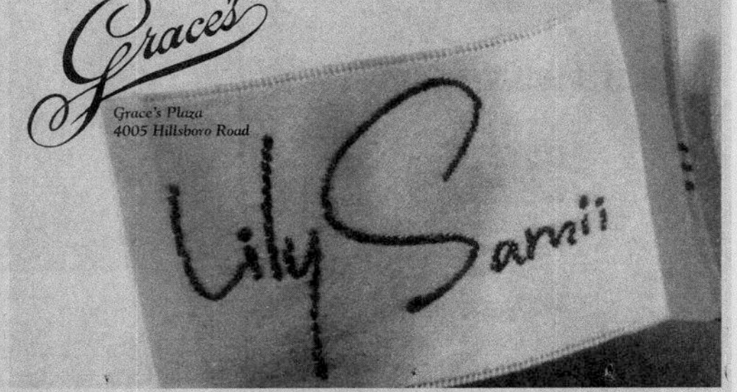

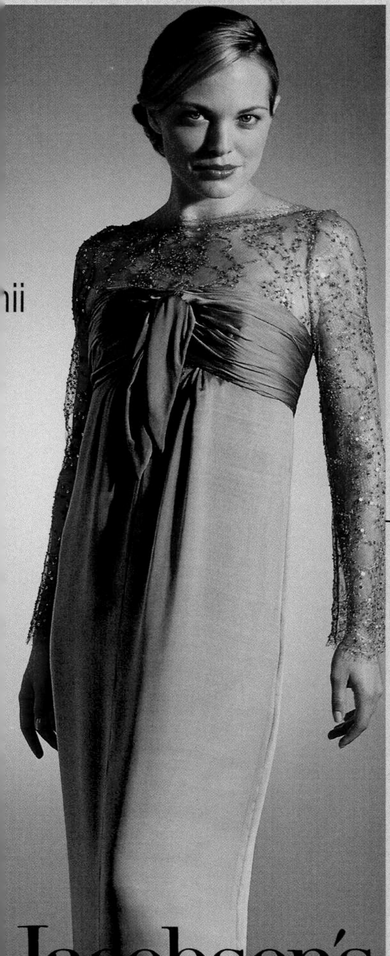

Jacobson's
www.jacobsons.com

Gowns

From page D1

(Gowns retail from $2,200-$8,000.)

Her biggest coup, however, was Stockton Street. From almost no recognition in the press, says the Iranian-born designer, she's now had 17 national and international publications write her up just in the past year, including a forthcoming spread in Town & Country.

"Coming to San Francisco was quite a big deal for me," says Samii, who since 1996 has also designed in collaboration with Jacques Patanzes, former head designer at Jean Patou.

"It's like moving from the country to the big city. Now I'm part of the city crowd and it's remarkable. I've always dressed people for the big openings, in a quiet way. Coming to San Francisco, everything gets so out there. People know what's going on in the fashion world. And they want to know more."

Like Michael Casey, Samii started out as a costume designer. Her career began in Hollywood, where she worked for the legendary Edith Head. She also interned in Paris with international couturier James Galanos. Samii, too, is known for her exceptional use of fabric: lustrous Thai and guipure silks, gossamer chiffons, subtle use of beading, crystals, appliqués, glittering buttons. Samii fans swear by the comfort of her cuts, and her ability to fit all body types. They love the fact that she'll often design in collaboration with a client to get just the right look and feel.

"Fuss is what I try to eliminate for the woman who wears my clothes," Samii says. "I think of all the problems you can have when you're dressed in a strapless gown or a dress that has sleeves: that you can't bend, can't move, can't drive. When my ladies put something on, it's zipped or buttoned and they're ready to go. They can forget about what they're wearing. That's what it's all about."

Reva Berelson from Tiburon agrees. Working closely with Samii, Berelson had her custom-design the ethereal strapless chiffon gown with matching stole and glittering abalone-shell neckpiece she'll wear to opening night of the San Francisco Opera on Sept. 11.

"When I put it on, I had chills," said Berelson. "It's so simple, yet so complex at the same time. The one thing most important to me is feeling special in something I wear. I know that when I go into an opening, I won't see someone wearing the same thing. In this gown by Lily, I know I will be unique."

Samii is attending the openings of the San Francisco Opera, and the forthcoming premier of San Francisco Opera's production of "A Streetcar Named Desire," where she will hobnob with such clients as symphony gala chairman Ann Moller Caen, Ann Otter from Belvedere (a Samii fan for more than 10 years), Loulie Sutro from Kentfield (a Samii collector for 27 years) and Nancy Stephens from Sausalito, just to name a few. "I'll be fussing with all my ladies," she said, as she adjusted Berelson's train for the umpteenth time.

Naturally Samii will be wearing her own designs. "But I don't know what I'll be wearing. I want everyone to pick up their gowns, first. I'll wear whatever is left over."

COVER STORY By Sylvia Rubin, Photography by Peter DaSilva

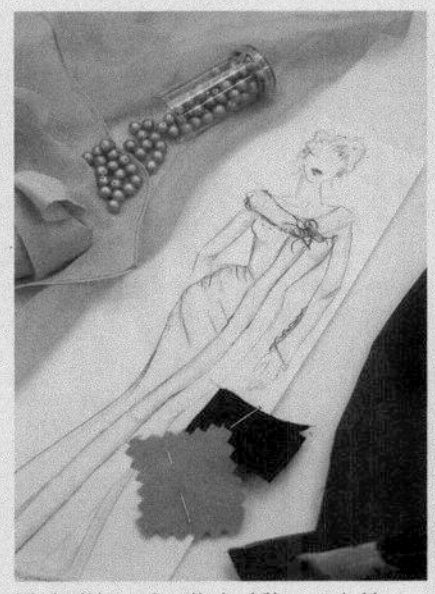

A sketch and fabric swatches and beads and ribbons are tools of the couture trade for San Francisco designer Lily Samii.

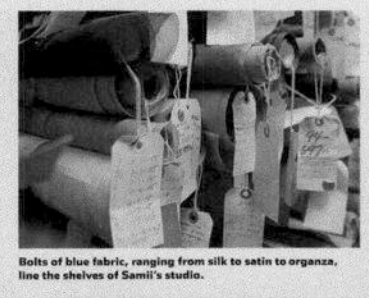

Bolts of blue fabric, ranging from silk to satin to organza, line the shelves of Samii's studio.

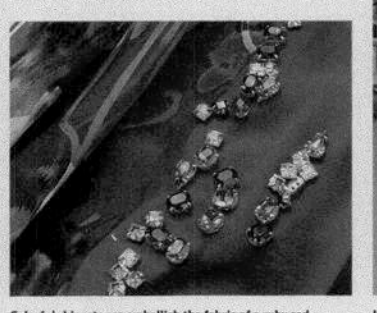

Colorful rhinestones embellish the fabric of a ruby red couture gown designed by Samii.

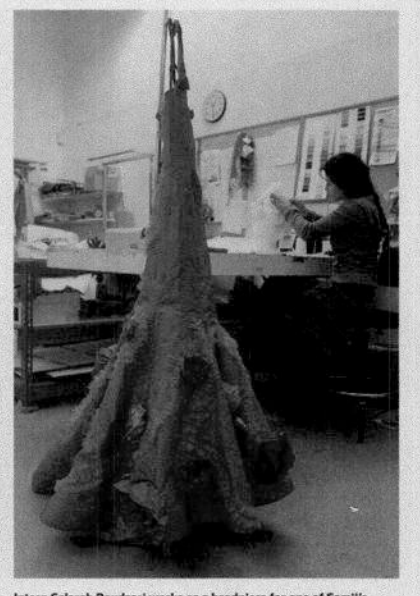

Intern Gelareh Roudsari works on a headpiece for one of Samii's gowns, such as this red taffeta design with handmade tulle flowers.

Haute couture creations — the top of the top of the line

The word "couture" is the most misunderstood term in fashion. It's become synonymous with high-end clothing and used incorrectly so often it's lost its meaning. Couture clothing is made to fit the client's body. Here in San Francisco, a handful of evening-gown and bridal designers, such as Lily Samii, Azadeh, Jin Wang, Colleen Quen, Christina Hurvis and Max Nugus to name a few, create one-of-a-kind couture suits and gowns made to fit each client's body.

But the true couture bluebloods are the the fashion houses that have been voted into the Chambre Syndicale de la Couture, founded in Paris by the great Charles Worth (an Englishman) in 1868, to preserve the art of haute couture ("high dressmaking" in French). These 10 fashion houses, and a handful of other designers who have been invited by the Syndicale, show their collections during Paris Haute Couture Week, which takes place every January and July.

The spring-summer 2008 shows will be held Jan. 21 to 24.

In 1939, there were 70 registered haute couture houses in Paris, including Chanel, Schiaparelli and Balenciaga. They have dwindled considerably, and include Givenchy, Dior and Christian Lacroix. But about 25 guest members, including Giorgio Armani, considered a foreign "corresponding" member, show during Paris Haute Couture week. (Armani made his haute couture debut — at age 70 — in 2005; and last January made fashion history by streaming his show live on the Internet).

Only a few hundred women in the world buy these clothes. A handful of local notables wear haute couture; including Ann Getty, Denise Hale, Dodie Rosekrans, Tatiana Sorokko, Dede Wilsey, Danielle Steel and Christine Suppes, former editor of Fashion-lines.com.

"Haute couture needs a champion," says Suppes, a regular client of John Paul Gaultier, Lacroix and the trio called On Aura Tout Vu. "Or it will go away."

True haute couture is a wildly imaginative, highly laborious form of dressmaking. Many of the ensembles are truly one of a kind, but others are made for more than one woman, although usually "not in the same country," said Marie Martinez Seznec, who was Lacroix's favorite model and now directs the designer's haute couture business. She was in town for the Lacroix San Francisco Ballet Auxiliary show last month.

These fanciful garments fuse fashion with costume. Artisans stitch crystals one by one onto tulle or silk; they make ornamental fabric flowers and hand-cover buttons in silk or velvet; the shoes, gloves and hats are made by hand. Made from yards and yards of the finest taffetas and satins, many are embroidered at the renowned House of Lesage. The designs are painted onto the fabric by hand, feathers, pearls and lace are meticulously applied. They are the most opulent, the most decadent fashion in the world. The inside of the garments are just as spectacular as the outside; the heavy silk or satin linings can stand alone as dresses; a cuff is lined with velvet that only the client can see and feel, a stiff, netted interior structure of a dress is as intricately constructed as a piece of architecture.

To qualify as a true haute couture fashion house, the staff must create both evening wear *flou* (the dressmaking) and day wear, *tailleur*, (the tailoring). There are specialized fitters and skilled workers for each. Precise measurements of the body — as many as 35 — are taken, and one to three fittings are required.

"They even measure your fingers," says Suppes.

Of course, these clothes are astronomically expensive. A day suit might cost $30,000 or more, an embellished evening gown $60,000 to $150,000, depending on the embellishment. (In comparison, a couture gown by a San Francisco designer ranges in price from about $2,500 to $10,000.)

"Some people buy cars or planes or boats, others buy art. I buy Lacroix. And one day, I will donate them to museums," Suppes says.

The local couturiers make gowns for women to wear to special events and the big galas in town. Like any couture gown, they start with measurements and a muslin (a prototype gown).

Azadeh, a longtime Bay Area couturier, has three Bay Area boutiques, including one on Union Square. The first floor of her stores carries her ready-to-wear line. But about 80 percent of her business is creating one-of-a-kind garments. Her local team of 22 tailors, embroiderers, beaders and lace applique artisans drape and embellish the fabric. "I dress a client for everything, from their vacations to their black ties. My strength is I know how to fit a woman; I know how to bring out the best of their bodies."

Max Nugus, who makes both couture and ready to wear, takes the traditional 35 or 36 measurements for his couture clients. He has shops in four cities, with a flagship store on Sutter Street. His most loyal client is the elegant arts patron Marcia Goldman, with whom he's worked exclusively for 15 years. He's made such diverse gowns for her as a hand-pleated sapphire blue strapless number with tiers of tiny pleats on the bodice, a hand-draped bias-cut skirt with additional pleating; and a bronze Art Deco-inspired hand-beaded gown with ribbons, sequins and lace.

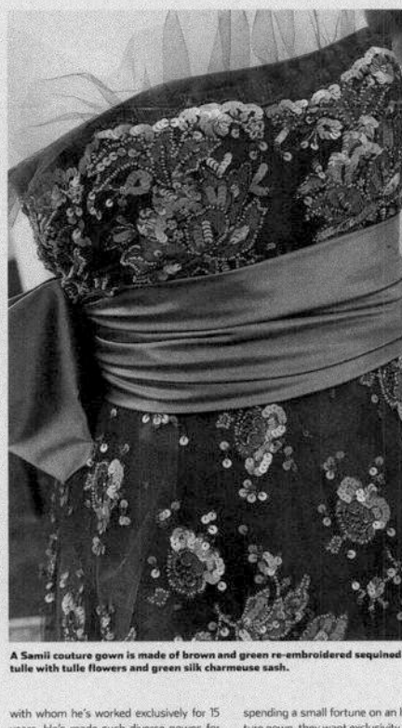

A Samii couture gown is made of brown and green re-embroidered sequined lace over tulle with tulle flowers and green silk charmeuse sash.

"I bring her samples, Marcia chooses, and then I remake the gown entirely for her body, and she's the only one who wears the gown to that particular event," he says. "We don't have to make a muslin anymore, but all the beading is done by hand upstairs at my shop."

Jin Wang takes about 35 measurements, she says, and much of the beading, lace applique and draping is done by hand. She has a bridal shop on Maiden Lane, and about 10 tailors at work at her South of Market workshop. When someone is spending a small fortune on an haute couture gown, they want exclusivity. But a truly one-of-a-kind gown is still a rarity. A movie star might wear your same haute couture gown on the red carpet; wealthy women in countries other than yours may have your gown.

"The big fiction about haute couture," says Wilsey, "is that it's only made for you. It isn't. They might make five of them. It's really ready-to-wear at higher prices." Still, she says, "the fabrics are spectacular, the sewing and the details are amazing; they are really beautiful things." Wilsey heads the Couture Circle for the Fine Arts Museums, a group of about 25 donors who love textiles and costumes and "come together to raise significant money" for fashion exhibitions.

Because of the hours and hours it takes to make these clothes, haute couture brings in no money to a fashion house, but their owners with deep pockets can afford to let their designers have their flights of fancy.

"Creating haute couture gives the mind unlimited oxygen," the French designer Lacroix, who is a member of the Syndicale, said by e-mail. Ralph Rucci, the only American to be invited to show his collection at the Paris haute couture shows, said that creating garments is the "most essential element" of dressmaking.

"Each garment in my haute couture collection is just one word of a huge paragraph," he said when reached at his New York atelier. "Once you show the runway collection, the paragraph makes sense."

A trip to one of these ateliers is all about lavish attention. "It's very homey at Lacroix; the dressing rooms are small and intimate; somewhat cooler at Gaultier, where you are being fitted in a much larger room," Suppes says.

Most women hold onto their haute couture forever, but not Ann Getty, who has worn Valentino, Givenchy, Saint Laurent, Ungaro and Balmain (by Oscar de la Renta) haute couture. "They are beautiful, but I consider them an important minor art," she said in a telephone interview. "They are clothes. You wear them and pass them along. I don't have any left in my closet."

You may be surprised to learn that storing these opulent creations is not a full-time job. Suppes uses the wide hangers that come with the gowns (to carry the weight of the beading). She stores her gowns in regular closets, but she does keep the lighting low. "My contractor wanted to put a skylight in my closet. I said, 'Are you crazy?' I had a window *removed* instead."

Wilsey confesses that her gowns "are so jammed together, they don't need hangers to stay up."

Hale's closet, where she mixes her haute couture and ready-to-wear clothing, is relatively neat and tidy. She stores some items, like a heavy ivory satin Gianfranco Ferre ball skirt with lavish beading and embroidery, in a white net garment bag. Hale, whose tiny frame has changed little over the decades, can pull out just about anything from her closet and it will fit perfectly.

"If you have a great fitter, you only need to have two fittings," says Hale, who was fitted for her first haute couture gown at Dior when she was just 19. "I learned a long time ago from the great fitter at Dior that all your clothes, not just couture, must fit right. But a great fitter will know what to take in and exactly where on your body to make you look slimmer, or in my case, taller. The fitter at Dior knew exactly how much needed to be taken in between the bust and the hips — I don't look 5-4 in a couture gown."

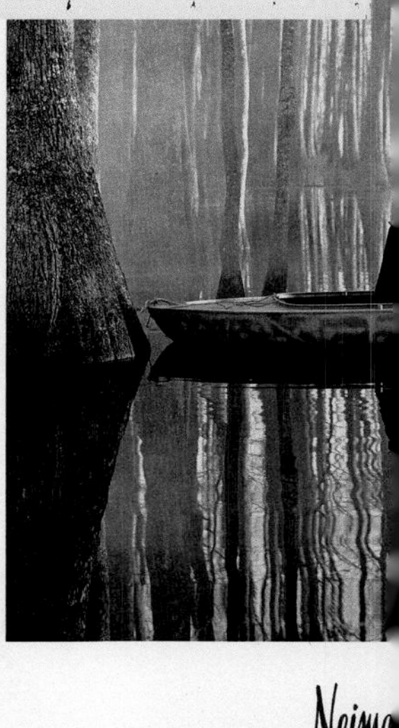

Neima…

San Francisco Chronicle
NORTHERN CALIFORNIA'S LARGEST NEWSPAPER
FRIDAY, NOVEMBER 7, 1997

S62

From N.Y. to Union Square

Lily Samii's designer salon to open here next month

Haute news: **Lily Samii**, who owns the popular L.Y.Z. boutique in Larkspur, is in New York to show her spring collection and to check with her architects about the salon she's opening on Union Square next month. Working with Lily on the salon and her collections: **Jacques Pantazes**, formerly resident designer at Jean Patou Haute Couture in Paris.

The spectacular Banana Republic flagship store was to celebrate its opening last night; lots of people, lots of Fishers and even a **Sue Fisher King** were expected. Also: swing music by the Recliners and rock by **Duncan Sheik**. Opening celebration gifts: linen coasters. "Totally cool," said one bright young thing, setting up the party.

The big Banana underwrote — totally cool — the Headlands Center for the Arts benefit last weekend. Among those there: **Randi** and **Bob Fisher**, **Cissie Swig**, **Diana Fuller**, the center's **Ella King Torrey** and artist **Ray Beldner** with wife **Catherine Clark**.

Van Kasper, who has just stepped down as the Exploratorium's board chairman after 17 years, knew that a few pals would be at a reception for him Tuesday at the Pacific-Union Club. What he didn't know was that the evening was a full-blown tribute to him. Item: The Exploratorium's new classrooms will be named for Van. **William Bowes** is now chairman.

Need tickets for the Rolling Stones in Oakland? **Jamie** **Dan McCall**. Ticket prices, negotiable. When she did i… on the Stones' last tour, she raised $25,000.

Regina Callan, an ABC-TV reporter in San Jose, recently took over Rococo Showplace to give a birthday party for her brothers, **Geoff**, 30, and **Bob**, 31, who live… L.A. Bob is a producer and Geoff has a role in "Frasier…

Gail Glasser celebrated her birthday Tuesday at a ve… healthy lunch given and prepared by **Tina Cella**, who claims to cook "without calories." "Divine," said **Sally Debenham** as she helped herself to more spinach ravio… Gail had had enough cream and butter last week in Pa… and Venice with her husband, **Dr. Harvey** . . . Chef **Michel Troisgros**, who does not claim to cook without calories, created a divine dinner in Paris for Friends of Vieilles Maisons Francaises. Among our friends there: **Marie-France de Sibert**, **Chandra** and **Robert Friese**, **Athena Troxel**, and **Martha** and **Proctor Jones**.

Souffles were served at the recent black-tie dinner p… ty celebrating the 40th anniversary of **John** and **Moniq…** **Gardiner**'s Tennis Ranch in the Carmel Valley. **Merv Griffin**, who divides his time between his valley home and his Beverly Hilton Hotel penthouse, entertained. "Where's the rest of the piano?" he asked as he sat dow… at John's Tom Thumb piano, which has 36 keys instea… of 88. They were just the ones Merv needed.

Kimberley Bakker is wearing a dazzling engagemen…

Symphony
Opera supporter…
go for bold…
statements, S.F…
designers on…
opening nigh…

local

Urban Lily

Lily Samii's San Francisco couture salon provides a civilized refuge from the hectic pace of downtown department stores. A discreet street-level entrance leads to a clean-lined, sun-splashed fourth-floor showroom overlooking Union Square. There Samii, a thirty-year veteran of fashion design and retailing, offers hand-finished special-occasion evening and daywear. Made of luxurious European fabrics, her clothes feature exquisite detailing. A favorite of such Bay Area residents as Danielle Walker and Peggy Haas, Samii strives for restrained elegance. Her collections—priced from $1,500 for a six-ply silk-crepe bias-cut dress with a crisscross back to $4,000 for an elaborate ball gown—are now designed with collaborator Jacques Pantazès, formerly of Jean Patou Haute Couture. These designs marry the fine aspects of couture with the needs of the American market. Says Samii: "My clothes are for the woman who understands chic without fanfare and over-styling." *260 Stockton St.; (415) 445-9505.* **MANDY BEHBEHANI**

Lily Samii

OOK
november

LIVING

Style

PROFILE | *Lily Samii*

The bold and the beautiful

Consumed by work, designer Lily Samii doesn't know about down time.

She's only half listening to her husband (he doesn't mind too much, she says) or her mother (she minds). Samii is always halfway out the door from her home in Marin to her San Francisco studio, where she puts in 12 or 15 hours a day on her eveningwear designs. "I'm always missing my exit on the freeway, I can't stop thinking about work," she says.

After 30 years in her small boutique in Larkspur, she took a chance, and moved to Union Square in 1997. It was like letting a bird out of the cage.

"For so many years, I kept all this stuff inside, I was afraid to experiment with my designs. I didn't have the guts," she says. "I kept thinking, will my clients understand what I'm trying to do with color? But now, I'm letting it all come out."

The 56-year-old designer, who is known for her ambitious color palette, risked losing some of her more conservative clients when she loosened up her designs, but she couldn't turn back. "The move was too much for some of my regular clients," she says, "but I've never felt more powerful or free."

Lily Samii

With a newfound confidence, she began to get bolder, pairing periwinkle with turquoise, red with bronze, raspberry with port, teal with purple. Her gowns tend to be fitted throughout the top, growing fuller at the hem. They often come with tulle petticoats and showoff linings in contrasting colors She likes to play with pleats, ruching and ruffles.

Last year, about half a dozen women wore her gowns to the Symphony and Opera openings; this year, the number has doubled. "Each person comes to me a blank canvas," she says, "and I watch them change right in front of my eyes; it's almost like I'm seeing a child born right in front of me."

Fashion has been a lifelong interest for Samii, who studied French dressmaking at a private girls' academy in Tehran, Iran. As an exchange student at UCLA, she worked part-time at Paramount's costume department under the tutelage of Oscar-winning designer Edith Head. She later interned with designer James Galanos.

In 1967, Samii headed north, and in 1969 opened LYZ, which sold her designs as well as ready-to-wear from the likes of Oscar de la Renta, Yves Saint Laurent and Bill Blass. She started a collection of day and evening separates in 1992, and an eponymous wholesale collection a year later. Finally, she made the move over the bridge, opening Lily Samii Collection in Union Square.

"I have no fear anymore," she says.

— *Sylvia Rubin and Laura Compton*

From left to right: Jacques Pantazes, Mark Rex, and Liz Schumacher

After subsequent trips to New York, Lily found herself in an interesting dilemma where everything was happening too fast. The Lily Samii label was presented in eighty top stores, including her own L.Y.Z. LTD. Her buying trips to Europe had shifted from buying ready-to-wear clothing to attending the fabric shows in Paris and Milan.

During this time, Lily hired a very talented designer and patternmaker by the name of Mark Rex, who had fallen into a difficult situation and had to close his business. This was serious now—Lily had a showroom in New York, a storefront in Larkspur, and a workshop in San Francisco.

The decision was made to close my beloved L.Y.Z. LTD on the eve of its thirtieth anniversary. It was an extremely emotional time for me, but the time had come. Meanwhile, a dashing young man came on board. Jacques Pantazes had moved back to San Francisco from Paris with a lofty resume, and I hired him. My team was shaping up to be an amazing group of young people, with Jacques and me at the helm.

I was reborn again! I had the excitement of a young person, even though I was nearly fifty years old at the time and had given up a very successful business for a whole new adventure! But it was exciting, and I was finally in my world of textiles and trims and everything that I had ever wanted.

Jacques and Lily in the showroom at 260 Stockton, San Francisco

I first met Lily at Première Vision in Paris during Fashion Week. I have only worked in haute couture, and that area of the event is not very crowded. It's amazing, you walk down the halls and you see John Galliano and other famous designers. Lily and I met there, and we had a cup a coffee with the art director of Jean Patou. Lily is funny because she has a recipe for the specific coffee she likes, and I just watched as she went through the fifteen directives to make her coffee. Lily knows what she wants and doesn't settle. I love that about her.

One day in Paris, I was looking through WWD and there was this ad and it says, "Lily Samii," and I was like, "OMG . . . THAT is Lily Samii—OMG! That's that lady who's so particular with her coffee??" I left Patou and worked for Dior and Chanel and I was spending more time in San Francisco. On one of my trips out west, I wrote Lily a letter. This is before email or cell phones. She wrote me a letter back, and said, "Come to my studio whenever you can," and so I did. I met with her and everything happened so organically. We clicked and the magic started immediately. I would send her designs and I would meet with her when I came back from Paris.

I moved to San Francisco and we started collaborating, and before I knew it, we were working together full-time. Because I came from haute couture, I brought to her a whole entire universe of things she didn't know about. I used French buttons and Italian silks, and Lily recognizes the best in the world. You put two threads in front of her and she knows which one is the best.

Once, we met at the airport and we showed up wearing identical outfits. Navy and cream striped sweater, navy blue slacks, same shoes. We looked like we called each other up to dress exactly alike! This is something that happened all the time! We are on the same wavelength.

I joined as her Creative Director, and I brought in a whole host of things that were not part of Lily Samii before, but were happening in haute couture. Haute couture is something so special.

I brought over the trims and techniques and added it to Lily's aesthetics. I came in with a menu of options of gowns, PJs, different types of pants. That is where the synergy happened, I don't think Lily considered that her career would move into making ball gowns with one hundred yards of silk and an explosion of beads.

Lily is a fabulous technician. She started as a fitter; her job was to make clothes fit. Being a fitter is an extremely challenging job, because she's dealing with a living, moving body that she has to dress and has to figure out how to allow the body to move. The body never stops moving and it heats up and gets cold. So, she would look at my designs and she could tell me what would work and what wouldn't. That is where the magic started to happen during our collaborations. We start doing these very conceptual things. The next question was, "This is great, but who's going to buy this?" And so we worked with Liz and Sarah who had a few accounts, but I wanted bigger and better accounts, so between all of us we grew the business to over eighty international accounts. Saks, Neiman Marcus, and every high-end boutique across the US, along with shops in Europe, Canada, and Mexico, carried our collection.

She bought the theater on Hyde Street and renovated it, and shortly thereafter we decided that L.Y.Z. LTD was not going to happen and we needed a salon in San Francisco. Lily wanted to be on Union Square, and nothing would stop her, and finally, a year-and-a-half later, she rents a space on Stockton Street. At the height of all this, we were pretty awesome and got a showroom on 7th Ave. in New York City.

If I wrote a book about us, it would be an epic novel or Hollywood musical. And, through all this we are still very close friends. She is like family.

—Jacques Pantazes

San Francisco Examiner

STYLE

S.F. Symphony *Opening Gala chair, Ann Moller Caen, sporting 200 carats of Cartier diamonds to set off her kelly green Lily Samii gown, gets an approving eye from Samii and designer Jacques Pantazes.*

Women are taking a fashion cue from men and looking more and more at 'bespoke' (made to measure) clothing

Gala season gets all-American start

TAILOR MADE

Gowns

From page D1

Gowns retail from $2,200-$8,000.)

Her biggest coup, however, was Stockton Street. From almost no recognition in the press, says the Iranian-born designer, she's now had 17 national and international publications write her up just in the past year, including a forthcoming spread in Town & Country.

"Coming to San Francisco was quite a big deal for me," says Samii, who since 1996 has also designed in collaboration with Jacques Patanzes, former head designer at Jean Patou.

"It's like moving from the country to the big city. Now I'm part of the city crowd and it's remarkable. I've always dressed people for the big openings, in a quiet way. Coming to San Francisco, everything gets so out there. People know what's going on in the fashion world. And they want to know more."

Like Michael Casey, Samii started out as a costume designer. Her career began in Hollywood, where she worked for the legendary Edith Head. She also interned in Paris with international couturier James Galanos. Samii, too, is known for her exceptional use of fabric: lustrous Thai and guipure silks, gossamer chiffons, subtle use of beading, crystals, appliqués, glittering buttons. Samii fans swear by the comfort of her cuts, and her ability to fit all body types. They love the fact that she'll often design in collaboration with a client to get just the right look and feel.

"Fuss is what I try to eliminate for the woman who wears my clothes," Samii says. "I think of all the problems you can have when you're dressed in a strapless gown or a dress that has sleeves: that you can't bend, can't move, can't drive. When my ladies put something on, it's zipped or buttoned and they're

ready to go. They can forget about what they're wearing. That's what it's all about."

Reva Berelson from Tiburon agrees. Working closely with Samii, Berelson had her custom-design the ethereal strapless chiffon gown with matching stole and glittering abalone-shell neckpiece she'll wear to opening night of the San Francisco Opera on Sept. 11.

"When I put it on, I had chills," said Berelson. "It's so simple, yet so complex at the same time. The one thing most important to me is feeling special in something I wear. I know that when I go into an opening, I won't see someone wearing the same thing. In this gown by Lily, I know I will be unique."

Samii is attending the openings of the San Francisco

Symphony, the San Francisco Opera, and the forthcoming premier of San Francisco Opera's production of "A Streetcar Named Desire," where she will hobnob with such clients as symphony gala chairman Ann Moller Caen, Ann Otter from Belvedere (a Samii fan for more than 10 years), Loulie Sutro from Kentfield (a Samii collector for 27 years) and Nancy Stephens from Sausalito, just to name a few. "I'll be fussing with all my ladies," she said, as she adjusted Berelson's train for the umpteenth time.

Naturally Samii will be wearing her own designs. "But I don't know what I'll be wearing. I want everyone to pick up their gowns, first. I'll wear whatever is left over."

ANN MOLLER CAEN will don this emerald green silk crepe gown by Jacques Pantazes of Lily Samii

260 STOCKTON STREET
SAN FRANCISCO

Lily decided that she needed a fabulous showroom in the heart of San Francisco, and, after months of searching, she found her dream space right on Union Square. She went on to hire one of the top architect firms in San Francisco, Brand + Allen, with Steve Lochte as lead architect. Lochte had just designed the Chanel store on Maiden Lane.

Haute Couture in San Francisco

Why not take the money you would spend on airfare and hotels in Paris and walk over to Lily Samii Collection at 260 Stockton Street on Union Square. Here you'll find a luxurious atelier filled with clothes and accessories that rival anything you'll see on Avenue Montagne.

Lily Samii has teamed up with some of the finest new talent from around the world. Together they are creating breathtaking day and evening wear in which exquisite couture workmanship is very much in evidence—handmade welted buttonholes; custom-boned bustiers; and rolled handkerchief hems; near invisible French seams; bias-cut gowns and dresses; reversible double-faced coats and jackets—all in the finest European couture fabrics.

The drill is the same is in Paris. You have a choice of seventy-five designs to consider. When your final choice is made, your measurements are carefully taken. You return for at least two fittings until the final garment is complete. Voilà! Haute Couture right here in San Francisco.

—*Clint Henderson*, MODA Magazine, *Winter 1997*

Lily Samii

Requests the pleasure of your company

at a cocktail reception

to celebrate the opening of

Lily Samii

C O L L E C T I O N
U n i o n   S q u a r e

Thursday, April 9
6:00 to 8:00 pm

260 Stockton, Fourth Floor
Union Square
San Francisco

R.S.V.P.: Betsy Linder
Gretchen De Witt
Diane Green
415/445-9505

Informal Modeling
Resort/Spring '98

Opposite page: Spring Collection, 2001

125 HYDE STREET
SAN FRANCISCO

"

I was on my way to the airport when the driver drove down Hyde Street. I was not at all familiar with that area. I was just looking around curiously when I noticed a funky art deco building for sale. I jotted down the address and soon I found myself to be the proud owner of a run-down historical building! 125 Hyde was the first movie theater in San Francisco.

I took Jacques to see the place. We both thought we have to have our first photo shoot there. The next fifteen years at 125 Hyde Street were an absolute blast.

"

Lily Samii's team was a select group of the most talented individuals in each of their respective fields. From seamstresses to merchandising pros, Lily only hired individuals with a stellar record of excellence. The Hyde Street location was her headquarters for creativity and production. There, the team of twenty-eight would make patterns, cut fabrics, hand-sew trims, create marketing plans, and work with retail accounts. They all worked together for years, and the group transformed into an international family.

The Hyde Street location was filled with excitement. They celebrated both happy and sad occasions—it never really seemed like work. Instead, there was always something going on, be it a baby shower or a retirement party. In January of 2003 they lost Mark Rex, then in August of 2015 they were again rattled by the untimely death of Zach Guinn.

Mark Rex
February 1956–January 2003

Zack Guinn
November 1973–August 2015

Traveling wardrobe, Fall 2000

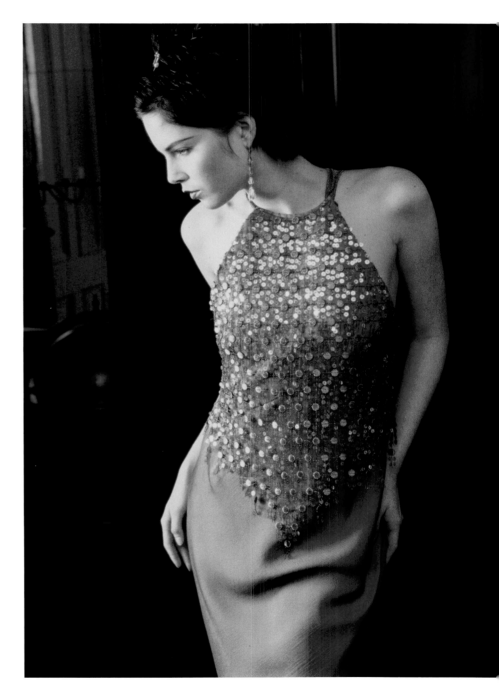

THE PRESS TAKES NOTICE

Lily's business took off and her collections were being requested at a feverish pace. Like Lily herself, her designs were classic and timeless. She pushed the envelope with colors and textures and her childhood influences of beauty and artistry found their muse in her craftsmanship.

Lily's distinctive designs are featured in the pages of society magazines being worn by San Francisco's elite at the many galas throughout the city. A true couture designer, each piece carefully made to fit Lily's client to perfection. Her designs are all crafted with exquisite fabrics and lace trims imported from Europe.

The press was quick to take note of Lily and her incredible work. Along with numerous *Nob Hill Gazette* covers of San Francisco royalty adorned in Lily Samii gowns, national magazines featured Lily Samii's work, including *Town & Country*, *WWD*, and *Vogue*. Multiple newspapers, including the *Herald Tribune* and the *San Francisco Chronicle*, prominently featured Lily's work, as well as did several television programs.

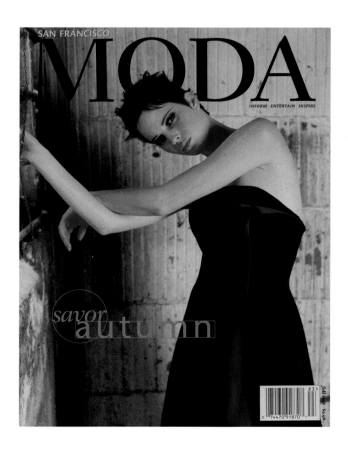

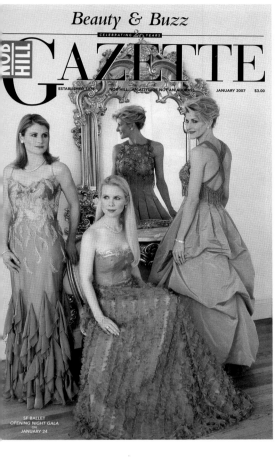

Beauty & Buzz

ᴺᴼᴮ ᴴᴵᴸᴸ GAZETTE

ESTABLISHED 1978   NOB HILL...AN ATTITUDE NOT AN ADDRESS   JANUARY 2007 $3.00

SF BALLET
OPENING NIGHT GALA
ON
JANUARY 24

On Your Toes…Galas Ahead

ᴺᴼᴮ ᴴᴵᴸᴸ GAZETTE

ESTABLISHED 1978   NOB HILL...AN ATTITUDE NOT AN ADDRESS   JANUARY 2008 $3.00

Savvy, Sleek & Stylish

ᴺᴼᴮ ᴴᴵᴸᴸ GAZETTE

ESTABLISHED 1978   NOB HILL...AN ATTITUDE NOT AN ADDRESS   MARCH 2009

GENTRY

JULY

**RETURN TO
ELEGANCE**
Gentry's Annual
Guide to
Luxurious Living

Elegant Jewels

**Collecting
Classic Cars**

GENTRY

SEPTEMBER

**GENTRY'S
FIRST
ANNUAL
STYLE
GUIDE**

**ELEGANT
FALL
FASHIONS**

RENEE SINGH
SEP '04   WWW.18MEDIA.COM
$4.99US

QUESTIONING ART
A look at the Cantor Center's
intriguing new show

GENTRY

SEPTEMBER

Divas of Fundraising
Local Women Who Make a Difference

The State of Real Estate
Peninsula Experts Discuss
the Housing Market

ANNE TAUBE AND
ESA MEDEARIS

LILY SAMII

The Cici Samii label

From the private collection of Mrs. Beverly Horn Maytag

From the private collection of Mrs. Beverly Horn Maytag

Jacques Pantazes and Lily Samii in the show room at 260 Stockton, San Francisco, 1998

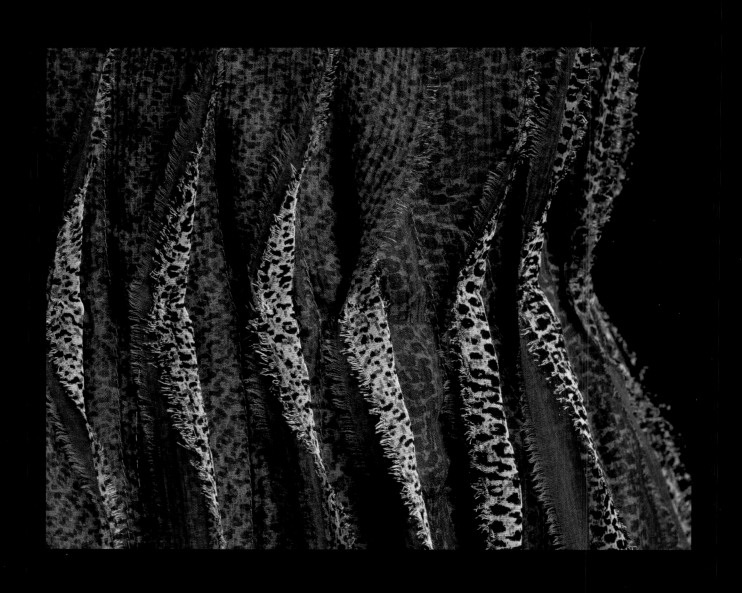

SHADES AND SILHOUETTES

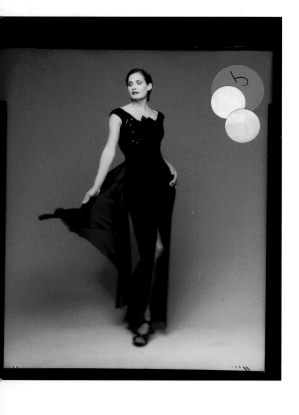

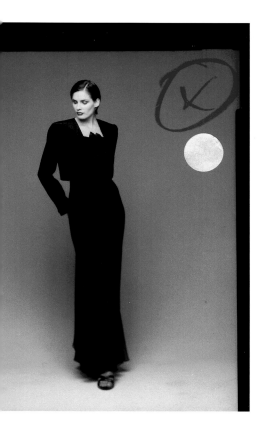

SAKS FIFTH AVENUE

B&W and Read All Over: Saks Fifth Avenue's windows feature the handiwork of local designer Lily Samii and the black and white gowns she has created for the 'Black & White Ball.' Real gowns are paired with faux couture gowns made from newspapers—The Wall Street Journal, Le Figaro, *and* Le Monde.

—*Rob Morse*, San Francisco Chronicle,
Friday, April 27, 2001

Samii

Saks Fifth Avenue display windows, Union Square, San Francisco, Spring 2005

15th Annual Tote Board

CELEBRATING 28 YEARS

GAZETTE
NOB HILL

ESTABLISHED 1978   NOB HILL...AN ATTITUDE NOT AN ADDRESS   JANUARY 2006 $3.00

Spring 2004

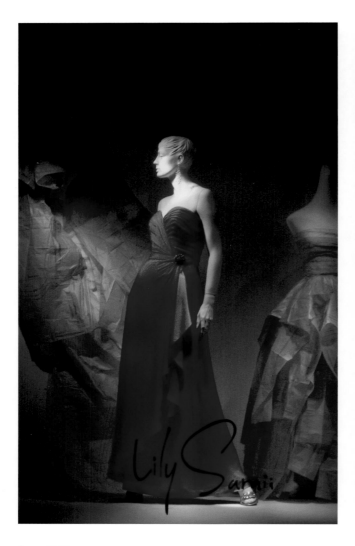

Spring 2005

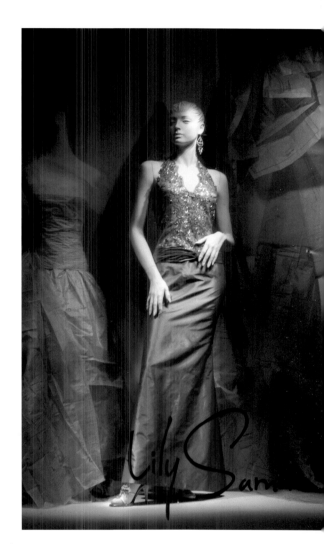

YOUR
FORTUNE

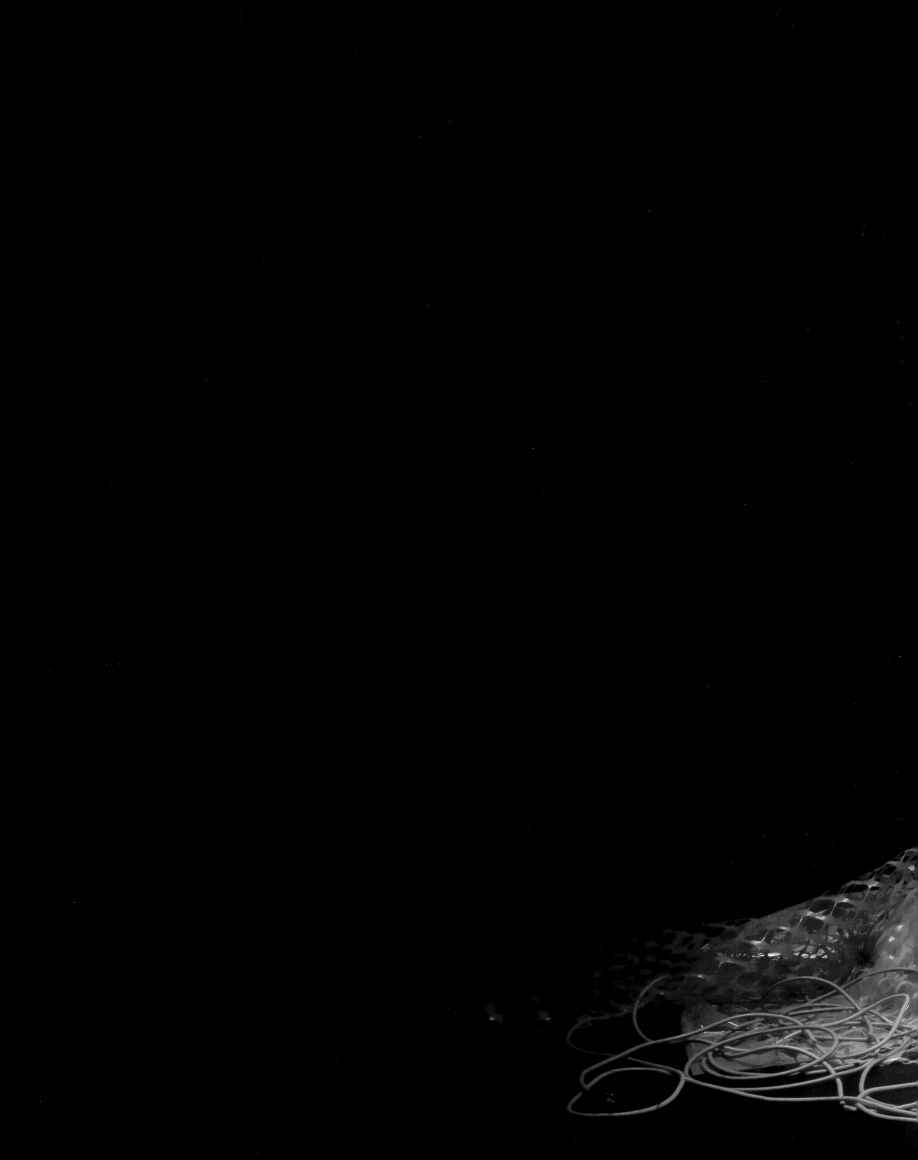

NOBILITY, CELEBRITIES, AND POLITICAL POWERHOUSES

For the next twenty years, Lily dressed women for every type of occasion on the planet. Her creations have been worn at epic events and locations, including royal weddings with kings and queens, the Presidential Inaugural Ball, the Senate, the White House Rose Garden, the Oscars, and audiences with the Queen of England. Lily dressed her ladies according to their events.

Jennifer Newsom, wearing a Lily Samii suit, with her husband Mayor Gavin Newsom (now governor of California) in January 2009

"Jennifer Siebel Newsom, who glowed in gossamer lavender—possibly the most stylish maternity gown ever."

SF Opera Opening-night Gala

Also cheering on home-team couture? Lily Samii, who celebrates twenty years as one of San Francisco's leading designing women.

Strategically positioned on the red carpet, Samii was a fashionable mother hen clucking as almost fifteen of her gowns nailed their sartorial marks. Including that of Jennifer Siebel Newsom, who glowed in gossamer lavender—possibly the most stylish maternity gown ever.

Ann Caen, another leading lady of style, agreed: "Jennifer looks amazing!"

"I'm really having fun tonight with Gavin, I keep calling him Governor Newsom," continued Caen, laughing. "I told him I'm practicing for his future."

—7x7 Magazine, *September 14, 2009*

Opposite page: first and second photos of Barbara and Richard Rosenberg with Queen Elizabeth at Buckingham Palace, ca. 1990; bottom photo of Barbara Rosenberg with Margaret Thatcher. Ensemble by L.Y.Z. LTD in all three

This page: top left is a magazine clipping including Barbro Osher, Honorary Consul General of Sweden in San Francisco, in the red gown, attending a Nobel Prize Award Ceremony in Sweden; top right: Diana Strandberg attending a Royal wedding in Jordan

Dear Lily and Laleh,

I wanted to thank you for the gorgeous dress that you created for my trip to Jordan for the Royal wedding celebrations. We had a wonderful time sightseeing throughout the country, including Petra, a truly amazing ancient city. We had an opportunity to meet some interesting people, including Queen Sophia of Spain, and the Farah Diba from your homeland.

Attached is a picture of your creation that I wore to the party in Aqaba. Believe it or not, this photo was taken after we had danced until 5 am—so I can attest that the dress was as comfortable as it was beautiful (which of course I can not say about my shoes. . . .).

I hope that you are well, and look forward to seeing you soon.

Fondly,
Diana Strandberg

Capital Chic: From Bay Area to Inauguration

Sen. Barbara Boxer has girlfriends, too, but she turned instead to San Francisco designer Lily Samii, who created a black, white, and gold beaded tuxedo jacket and black fishtail skirt for the gala. Samii is dressing several other Bay Area women, including Napa Valley vintner Shari Staglin, who will wear a violet silk crepe strapless gown with side gathers and matching organza ruffle jacket (Staglin wines will be served at some of the inaugural events), and Barbara Engmann, who will wear an anthracite and sapphire silk Duchess strapless gown with beaded hand embellishment.

Not mentioned in the press, but also attending the inaugural events wearing Lily Samii were:

Marissa Meyer of Google, who wore a red and black chiffon printed gown.

Candy Robertson with her husband, Peter, Vice President of the Board of Directors of Chevron Corp, who wore a brown lace over blush bustier with a long brown silk and wool skirt.

—*Sylvia Rubin*, San Francisco Chronicle, *Sunday, January 18, 2009*

This page, above: Barbara Engmann; below left: a note from Kansas Senator Nancy Kassebaum; below right: Napa Valley vintner Shari Staglin

Opposite page, top left: Christina Decker with President Bill Clinton; right three: Lily and Mark Samii at the White House attending a Rose Garden wedding; bottom left: Lily casually making a phone call in Lincoln's bedroom

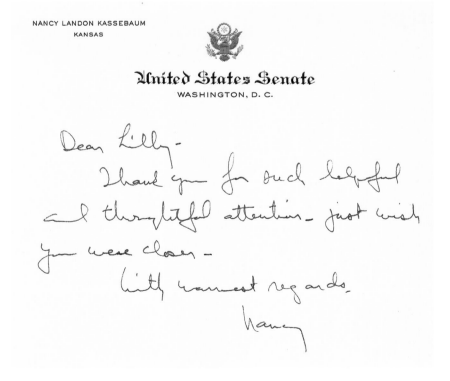

NANCY LANDON KASSEBAUM
KANSAS

United States Senate
WASHINGTON, D. C.

Dear Lilly—
Thank you for such helpful and thoughtful attention — just wish you were closer —
With warmest regards,
Nancy

BARBARA BOXER

For many of my big happenings, Lily made the clothes I wore. Every happy event between 1975–1995, Lily made my outfits. She designed an elegant dress for my son's wedding. She created a beautiful suit I wore when I marched up the steps of the Capitol for Anita Hill's hearing. The happiest moments in my life happened to be when I was wearing something from Lily Samii. I was wearing her creation when shaking Ronald Reagan's hand. The first time I ever met a president was when I was wearing a Lily Samii dress! And the night I won my senate race, I was in Lily Samii. Another piece was a teal green suit that I wore for my swearing-in to the Senate. I have one beautiful gown when I went to the Oscars . . . I still have it. Lily was involved in all these amazing occasions. I have saved all the outfits Lily has made me and I wear them all! People ask me and I say, "It's twenty-five years old!"

When I decided not to run for Senate, I was feeling nostalgic and I called Lily to let her know that I was retiring. She said, "Come over!" We chatted, and then she offered to make me a pantsuit for Hillary Clinton's nomination during the Democratic Convention. It was a beautiful blue suit that is on my Twitter page. Lily is just a part of my life. She has been there for all the biggest moments in both my personal and public life.

—Barbara Boxer

Pictured left: Senator Barbara Boxer, Lily Samii, and First Lady Hilary Clinton

To Lilly -
with love,
Barbara
1997

Above, left: Vice President Al Gore, and Senator Barbara Boxer

Above, right: Senator Barbara Boxer and Lily Samii

Left and below: A letter to Lily from Barbara Boxer referring to the photo below of her with President Ronald Reagan

BARBARA BOXER
6TH DISTRICT, CALIFORNIA

Congress of the United States
House of Representatives
Washington, D.C. 20515
February 13, 1983

LYZ Limited
1020 Magnolia Avenue
Larkspur, CA 94939

Dear Lily:

Enclosed is a photograph that was taken the evening I had dinner at the White House with President Reagan.

Of course, the dress was absolutely lovely.

I send my best to you!

In friendship,

BARBARA BOXER
Member of Congress

BB/mel

Here it is!

Rita Moreno

Lily Samii

Above and opposite: Oscar, Emmy, Grammy, and Tony award-winner Rita Moreno wearing a dress by Lily Samii, arrives at The Heart Truth Red Dress show during Mercedes-Benz Fashion Week–Fall 2008 on February 1, 2008, in New York City.

Above: Rita Moreno posing with Liza Minnelli and Barbara Bush

Lily created an original design for Denise Hale of San Francisco. It was a graceful, nearly weightless black and ivory gown. The perfectly domed skirt was made of multiple layers of silk gazar, silk organza, and crisp tulle, and finished with a top layer of shooting jet thistle and silk ivory Japanese anemone flowers. At the heart are touches of copper, just like the foil that graces the Époque Cuvée bottle. Lily joined Mrs. Hale to attend the festivities in Épernay, France.

If I could use one word to describe this gown, it's longevity.

—Denise Hale

Above: Denise Hale attending the 100th Anniversary of Perrier-Jouët's Belle Époque Cuvée, also known as the Flower Bottle, in Épernay, France, 2002

Opposite: Denise Hale attending the San Francisco Opera's Opening Night Gala, 2015

I met Lily in 1992 when I had an interview with the State Board of Accountancy. I was a working mom living in Marin and I had no time to shop or look for quality clothes that could take me from day to evening. All of my friends were talking about this store L.Y.Z., which was hard to find because it was tucked away on a random street in Larkspur. And when I finally found it, it was like walking into a style icon fairytale. I just started my own business and I didn't have much money to spend on clothing. So, when I first went into L.Y.Z., I was looking at the prices and I was hoping to be able to afford just one or two of the beautiful pieces of clothing in the boutique. Later, when my career got more lucrative, I would go in and choose much more for my wardrobe. Lily carried an impressive line of designers and always had pieces that were high-quality, very professional, and very flattering that I could go from work to date night with my husband. One of the many qualities that make Lily so special is that she gets to know her clients—

what makes them happy, what flatters them, and looks great on them. And Lily would hand-select pieces for me after asking a series of questions and getting to know what I needed the outfit for and the appearance I wanted to convey. And, by the way, I did get the position with the State Board of Accountancy, and I believe that part of it was because I felt confident and strong in the suit Lily chose for that the occasion. I knew when I wore clothing hand-selected by Lily that I would feel better and I'd be more confident. She had terrific style and staff. I became a loyal fan of Lily. When a client would go into her boutique, she would immediately start asking questions—interviewing clients became Lily's hallmark. She would ask about what they were dressing for and how did they want to feel. I had to be comfortable in my clothing because I was sitting for hours and had to be professional. Lily's selections were very professional yet very feminine. She had a great reputation for her selections of fabrics, style, and colors. I knew that Lily wanted me to be happy and to look great. She takes this all very personally and she wants everyone to look amazing. In 1996 my son had his bar mitzvah and Lily made my dress for me. I remember it like it was yesterday. It was a beautiful champagne color that made me feel festive.

—Diane Rubin

TEXTURES AND THREADS

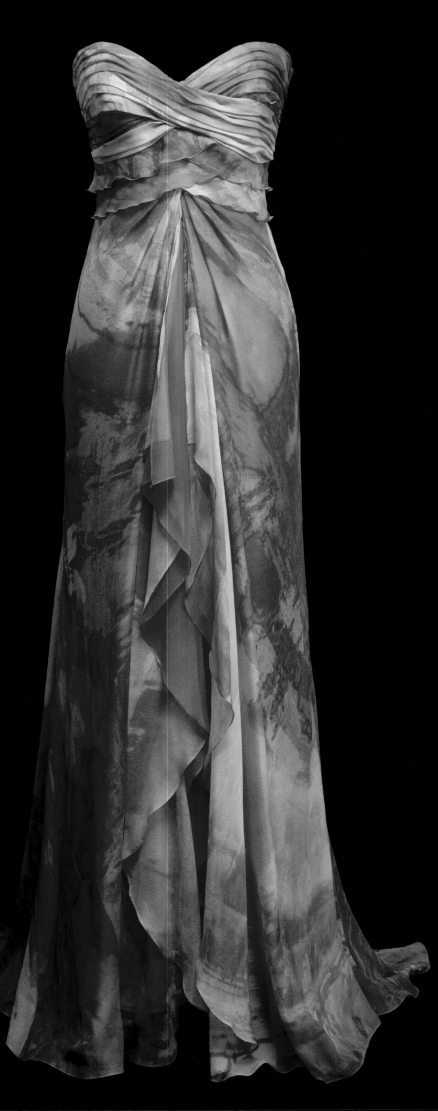

THE 2010 FOOD ISSUE

TASTE THE FUTURE: The new wave of brilliant kitchen iconoclasts poised to rock the restaurant world   **THE BEST CHEFS:** Four local talents who own this moment
A TERROIRISTE'S PLOT: Vintner Randall Grahm isn't joking this time   ALSO: 70+ reviews

SanFrancisco

$4.95 August 2010
www.sanfranmag.com

MODERNLUXURY

PRECISELY UNPRETENTIOUS:
Dishes like this one—beet soup with a purée of unripe pickled strawberries, garnished with young root vegetables and flowering herbs—put James Syhabout, of Commis, on cuisine's leading edge. SEE PAGE 60

Separate but equal

The recession has inspired a cadre of designers to bring back versatile separates. Now **Lily Samii**, whose custom gowns dominate the S.F. gala scene, has joined the fray.

BY JOANNE FURIO
PHOTOGRAPHED BY LAURA FLIPPEN

Lily Samii's career reads like a movie pitch: UCLA college girl trained in French dressmaking in Tehran is hired by a posh boutique to do alterations. Her big break comes when she remakes part of a gown for actress Joan Blondell. This leads to an internship with the legendary Edith Head at Paramount, then another with the esteemed James Galanos. Migrating north in 1969, she opens a Lockspur boutique that grows into a fashion house and moves into a bona Union Square atelier in 1998, enticing generations of socialites and buyers at Saks. But there's a sequel to the Hollywood ending: A global downturn and designer Phoebe Philo's paradigm-shifting spring collection for Céline draws fashion's attention back to basics—fine fabric, quality workmanship, and enduring styles, all among Samii's trademarks. So now she has introduced a ready-to-wear line of separates—the antithesis of H&M and Uniqlo—for the fast-fashion generation. We got a first look at her second coming. BY APPOINTMENT, 255 DIGGITOM ST., 4TH FL., S.F., 415-362-0626, LILYSAMII.COM

What led you to start a ready-to-wear line after more than 40 years in the business? We've always made custom daywear, and we are keeping the same level of integrity in ready-to-wear, as far as fabrics and workmanship are concerned. But the streamlined styles appeal to younger women. »

In her Harte Street studio, Lily Samii sketches designs for her new collection of separates.

42 SAN FRANCISCO AUGUST 2010

From left: innovative laser-cut circle-disc fabric; Samii sketching; a rack of samples from her 2010 resort ready-to-wear collection.

Your pink coat with the standup collar and three-quarter-length sleeves is so Jackie Kennedy. Why is that silhouette still fresh today? It has the simplest lines. There is no gimmick. Design doesn't have to be complicated to be fabulous.

One of the high-tech fabrics you use is made up of small circles on a mesh background, creating a fish-scale effect. What's innovative is that a laser cuts the fabric and seals it at the same time, so there's no fraying around the edges. It is incredible.

I'm happy to see you're doing a high-waisted trouser. I couldn't wait to say farewell to the hip-hugger, which only looks good on the young and narrow. I have been doing the same pant since I started. It looks good on 90 percent of people.

You're also showing asymmetrical necklines. Will that continue into fall? I am the wrong person to talk to about trends, because I don't believe in them. The asymmetrical neckline has existed since the ancient Egyptians. It will always be around. It is a flattering neckline for a lot of women.

What else should women in San Francisco wear this fall? What are the key pieces? Duster coats with varying sleeve lengths and wool jersey or wool crepe dresses with a loose drape are most important. Depending on one's body, they can be worn belted or loose. The unexpected folds of fabric make the dresses body-friendly for any age.

Speaking of trends, are there some you despise? Big shoulder pads in the '80s—I hate them with a passion. They made people look so weird. The '80s were the worst: big shoulders, big hair, too much of everything.

What can we expect from your fall 2010 ready-to-wear collection, debuting at Saks? Besides experimental fabrics, I'm using highly engineered shapes, metallic threads, and special treatments like embossing to play

with light, but keeping our house's prim and classic designs. Colors will range from copper and burnt sienna to pewter and steel to patent and matte black.

How do you get young women who are used to McFashion to appreciate or understand quality? Education, education! Believe me, it's not easy—I am always promoting that concept. I feel it's my calling to make sure that young people realize quality is far more cost effective and attractive, and it has a much longer shelf life.

Do you subscribe to the theory of keeping everything, because it will eventually come back? If it is classic, it should never go out of style. Only keep pieces that look good on you and that you're going to wear over and over.

Whose ready-to-wear do you buy, and why? A lot of my pants are Dior because they fit well. I also like Chanel jackets and pants because they are easy to wear, both in terms of fit and classic styling.

You're originally from Iran. Did that trigger your love affair with color? I've always loved color. I guess it's just something I was born with.

Yet you're wearing head-to-toe black. I do because I'm lazy. I don't want to think in the morning. I don't want to think when I'm traveling. I have a black T-shirt in every fabric, from cotton to cashmere.

How did you end up with such an urban look, having lived most of your life in sunny California? I used to go on buying trips to New York in the '70s, and the women were all wearing black dresses and pearls and red lipstick. I wanted to look like them, and it stuck with me. ■

Samii says

Five separates that will spiff up your look.

1. A pair of well-fitting pants: "Preferably wool crepe, which transcends the seasons."

2. A novelty jacket: "I love it in bright, strong colors. Wear it with a simple dress or pants, and let the jacket do the talking."

3. A fitted skirt: "In navy, not black, continuing our nod to color. This can be paired with..."

4. ...a crisp white blouse: "My favorite in the ready-to-wear line is made of pure white silk shantung with organza sleeves."

5. A novelty top: "We have one that has a chiffon cowl-back T-shirt design, and the fabric is covered in flat paillettes, a type of sequin, giving it a unique look. Wear it to the office with a navy skirt or out to a nightclub with a pair of jeans and heels—heads will turn!"

Resort Spring 2010 Collection

ON THE RUNWAY

SF iS

FEBRUARY
2008

A fine romance:
Lily Samii's fashionable affair

LUST-WORTHY GIFTS

BEST TIPS FOR LUXURIOUSLY SOFT, KISSABLE LIPS

DRAWN TOGETHER — ILLUSTRATOR CREATES FANCIFUL DOSSIER FOR HERMES

Here comes the bridal gown, fitted to perfection

In her Hyde Street studio: Designer Lily Samii (above right) and Minkyoung Kim, a designer/patternmaker, put finishing touches on a strapless, ruched tulle wedding gown embroidered with feathers and tulle bows. Samii has a staff of 15 working to help create her couture garments.

COVER STORY By Sylvia Rubin

Black silk chiffon and silk crepe cocktail dress with organza flower and organza shoulder strap.

Ice-blue duchess satin strapless gown with lace bodice detail.

Short black-and-white print gazar cocktail dress with sequined collar.

White silk crepe column gown with black sequin trim and flower.

Samii keeps with tradition in charity show

One of the biggest charity fashion shows in town — playing to more than 1,000 guests — kept up with tradition this year when San Francisco designer Lily Samii showed her luxe cocktail and evening wear collection for the Girls' Town of Italy's 45th anniversary show and luncheon in December at the Fairmont Hotel.

A special presentation was made to longtime Girls' Town supporter Bella Farrow, the general chairwoman of the charity for 15 years. Sherlee Rhine of 77 Maiden Lane was also honored for her years of donating hair and makeup services to the show. After a short speech expressing her gratitude, Farrow took a congratulatory walk down the long runway to much applause.

Then came the models, wearing satins and silks from Samii's spring 2008 Supernova collection. After an opening series of black-and-white numbers, the colors showed up: hot pink, citron, tangerine, ice blue and ice pink. In addition to the traditional duchess satin, silk crepe and silk chiffon gowns, Samii showed others with the added pizzazz of burnout silk chiffon, embroidered shantungs and embellished laces.

Many in the audience — longtime Girls' Town advocates — had never heard of Samii. Girls' Town of Italy was founded in 1956 (11 years after Boys' Town of Italy) by actress Linda Darnell, who, while making a movie in Rome, was moved to help impoverished young girls by setting up housing and educational programs.

Girls' Town supporter Bobbie Vannucci, a former real estate agent, has come to these events for 25 years. She had no idea who this Lily Samii was, although she's probably walked right by Samii's Union Square studio a million times on her way to and from Neiman's or Saks. It's more or less hidden from view, upstairs inside a Stockton Street office building that also houses Bibbo hair salon and the Style Paris showroom.

"I'd never heard of her. I had no idea what to expect," Vannucci, who hails from Walnut Creek, said after the show. "But there was this lavender-green cocktail dress with stitching down the back that I loved. ... Now that I've seen what she does, I'm going to her showroom as soon as I get the chance."

Samii said she stretched herself with this collection, experimenting with adding multiple curvy seams for a sexier silhouette. "It's new for me to do so many seams, but I love the way the dresses move and how they fit the body," she said a few weeks earlier, in her atelier.

Some standout looks included an ice-blue duchess satin gown with pleated satin belt, a sea-mist strapless gown with bias cut tulle strip hem, a lilac taffeta dress with pleated collar, and the grand finale dress, a showstopper strapless ivory organza bridal gown with multiple pleated panels at the bodice and a 9-foot train made of organza over layers of tulle.

Designer Lily Samii works on a custom couture gown at her San Francisco design studio.

Ivory cellophane striped organza bridal gown with pleated neckline, empire belt and long tulle and organza train.

The fashion show was in honor and celebration of Hospice By The Bay, a charity near and dear to my heart. Their commitment and service to our community resonated with my philosophy of contributing to the welfare of others.

Lily Samii and the models after her fashion show at the Four Seasons Hotel, San Francisco, 2008

FASHION

The long and short of Samii

By Sylvia Rubin
CHRONICLE FASHION CORRESPONDENT

Is that a pair of shorts on the runway?

Showing shorts at a spring fashion show is hardly a stop-the-presses moment. On the other hand, for longtime San Francisco designer Lily Samii, who's known for evening wear, the three-piece silk charmeuse aqua and green print shorts outfit that opened her most recent runway show was indeed a big deal. When she was dreaming up ideas for her new collection of watercolor-print coats and lime-green, pink and ocean-blue dresses and gowns — inspired by a recent cruise to Turkey — Samii went through the ifs, ands and buts in her head: "No, no. I'm not known for shorts. ... But yes, I can be known for that. Why not? It's an evolution. You can't get stuck in a rut."

Samii continues on N3

model presents a Lily Samii gown with a train with handmade rosettes on tulle from
08 at a 13-piece retrospective benefit for the Bay Area Arthritis Auxiliary.
e jewelry is by Kate Horan of Sorelle Bionde.

FROM THE COVER

The long and short of local designer's 20-year career

Samii from page N1

While so many businesses have come and gone, Samii has survived and thrived for 20 years.

"This is my third recession," said the soft-spoken designer. "I've had to cut back my wholesale business 50 percent in the last two years. I closed my New York showroom in 2004. But when the stores cut back on inventory, it pays off for someone like me because I get new customers who still need evening wear."

They include many of San

> **"When I look at some of my older gowns now, I still think they're gorgeous, but they are too stiff."**
>
> *Lily Samii, designer*

Francisco's most prominent arts patrons, like Karen Caldwell, who consistently wears Samii's expertly draped and beaded gowns to black-tie gala affairs. Even 10 years ago, evening wear meant a big, stiff ball gown with matching shawl. "There are no shawls in the collection today," Samii said.

An Iranian native who came to the United States as an exchange student (and interned with Edith Head and James Galanos, no less), Samii began her own career here in the '70s running a successful upscale boutique in Larkspur, selling gowns by Oscar de la Renta, Valentino and others, as well as her own designs.

Around her 50th birthday she switched gears, opening her own Stockton Street atelier in 1997, where she remains today. Last week, her retrospective fashion show, held at the Westin St. Francis, which included 13 pieces from 1999 to 2009, raised more than $200,000 for the Bay Area Arthritis Auxiliary. Samii's line is carried at Saks Fifth Avenue Union Square.

Over the years, her style has undergone a slow, steady change. Her cocktail dresses are made of lighter, stretchier fabrics, and she's using digital prints, laser-cut details and less beading overall. What hasn't changed is Samii's sense of color play — she isn't afraid of hot pink or chartreuse; she might line a low-back bronze sequined cocktail dress in deep violet.

"When I look at some of my older gowns now, I still think they're gorgeous," Samii said, "but they are too stiff, too fussy — they don't have a place in today's wardrobe."

Even worse than fussy: Many designers don't want to be known as someone who dresses mothers of the bride. But this is one of Samii's specialties, and the women return to her for dresses and suits for other occasions.

Carol Doll, a trustee of the Arthritis Foundation Northern California Chapter, who was at the show, is one of them.

"This show was all about Lily being unafraid and unabashed."

E-mail comments to style@sfchronicle.com.

Photos by Laura Morton / Special to The Chronicle

Lily Samii fixes the first looks on her models backstage at the Westin St. Francis before the fashion show while Hillie Yung from Saks Fifth Avenue applies makeup.

Samii's designs have evolved from structured gowns to simple yet elegant pieces such as, at left, silk stained glass laser-cut circle dress (left), aqua silk charmeuse jacket, acid pear tank and stained glass shorts (right), and at far right, ruffled-sleeve top with navy taffeta bubble skirt.

HEART AND SOUL

My soul is so connected to the delicate artwork of hand embroidery. In moments when I would find myself stressed out, I'd find solace in carefully sewing beads, sequence, pearls, and stones on gowns with a steady eye and focus. Embroidery is my therapy and work like this calms me.

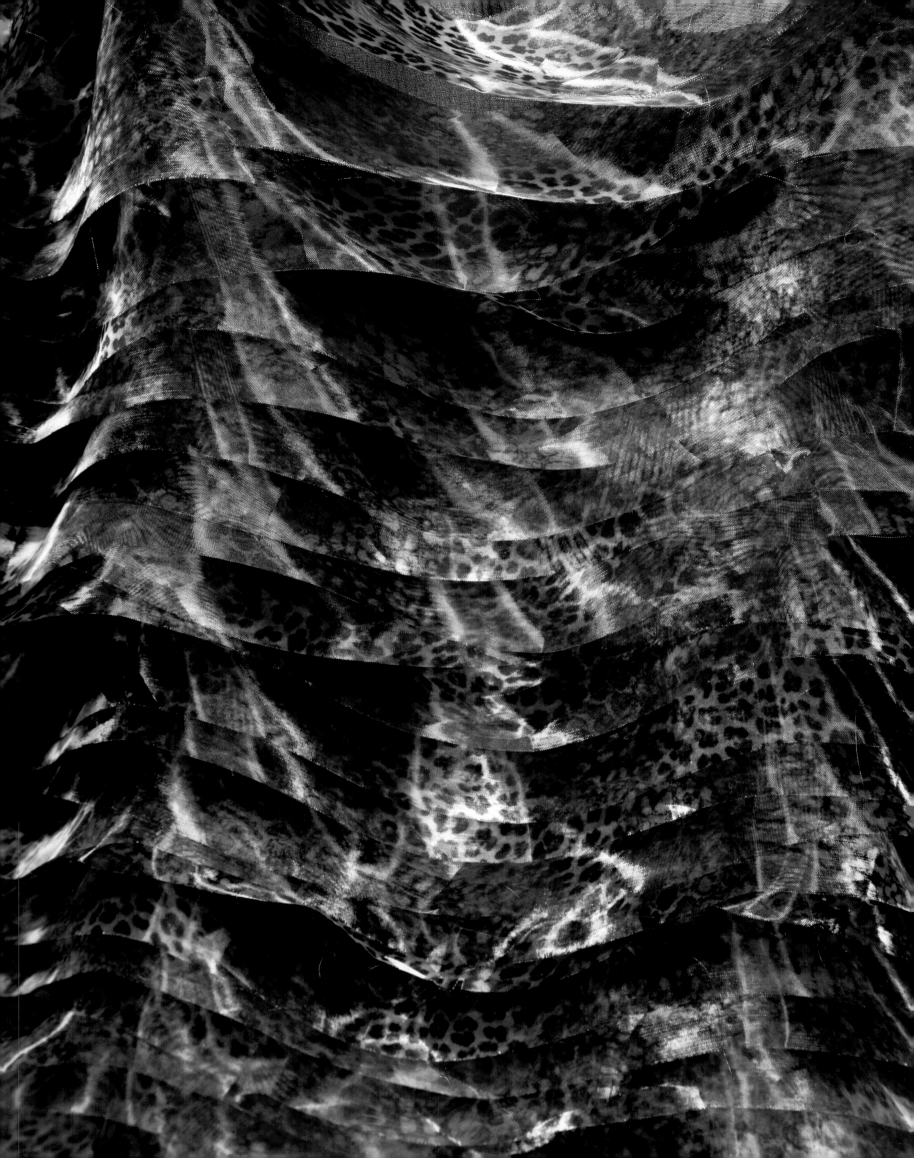

Gypsy Bride, Fashion Week 2005

From the private collection of Mrs. Diane Rubin

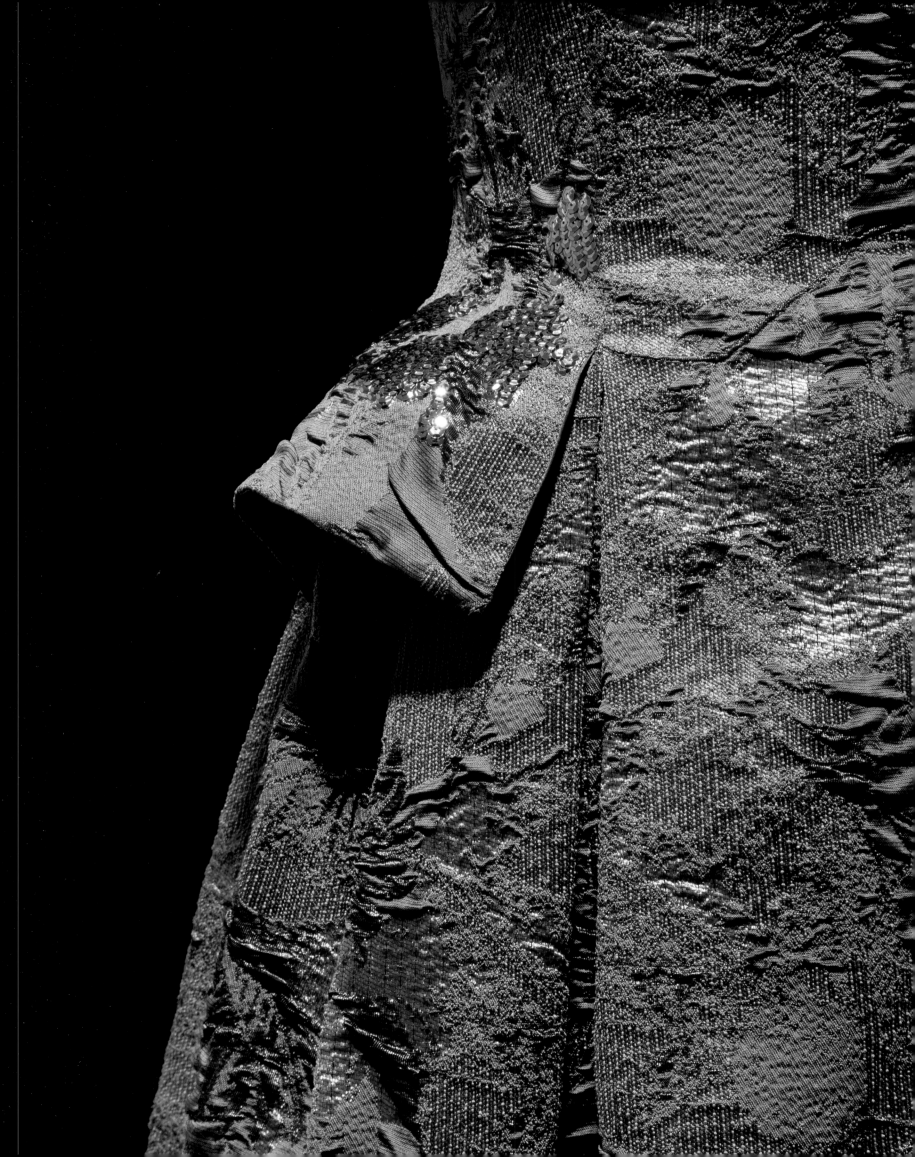

From the Private Haute Couture Collection of Lily Samii

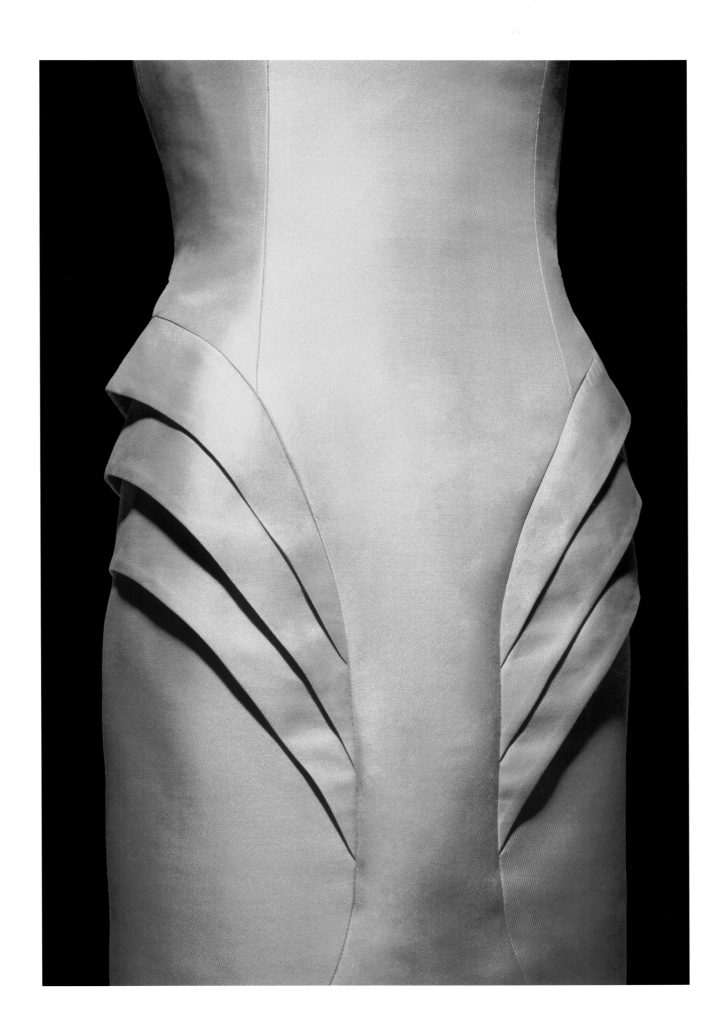

Spanish Bride, Fashion Week 2006
From the Private Haute Couture Collection of Lily Samii

From the private collection of Mrs. Alison Hall Mauzé

From the Private Haute Couture Collection of Lily Samii

From the Private Haute Couture Collection of Lily Samii

From the private collection of Mrs. Melodie Batt Rubin

RED CARPETS AND GALAS

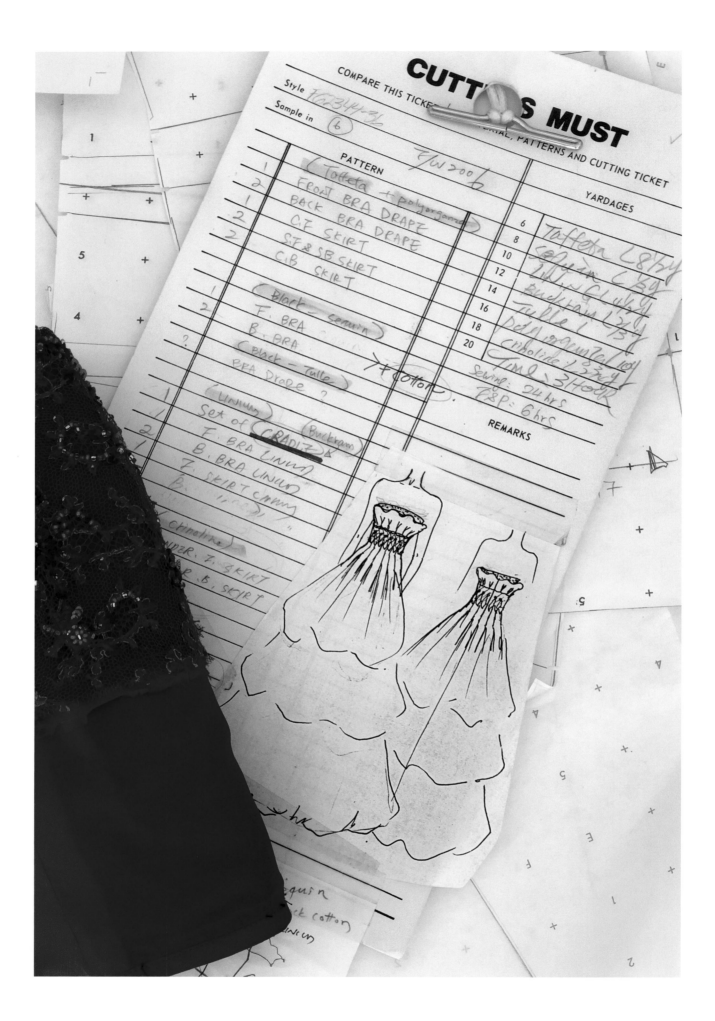

From left to right: Courtney Labe in blue, Maryam Muduroglu in yellow, and Kate Shilvock in red, all wearing Lily Samii gowns to the San Francisco Opera Opening Night Gala, September 8, 2017

It was a very special time in my life. I was the president of the Opera Guild and I knew that the only person who could make me a gown fitting for the occasion was Lily Samii. I spoke with Lily about what I wanted, what I would be happy wearing, and what would work for my style and frame. Lily started sketching! She created four or five different sketches for me, and we discussed each one in detail until we both agreed on the design of this magnificent gown. Once we chose the gown, Lily worked on the color combinations. She has just exquisite tastes and understanding for color that are really out of the ordinary. I often wear one of her specially-designed pieces and people will come up to me and say, "Oh that must be a Lily Samii."

—Diane Rubin

Opposite page: Diane Rubin wearing a Lily Samii gown to the San Francisco Opera Opening Night Gala, September 6, 2013

The late Charlot Malin and Mary Poland, both wearing a Lily Samii gown to the San Francisco Opera Opening Night Gala, September 2010

Oh, so many of my favorite moments have happened when I was in a Lily Samii gown! I will never forget the first time: Lily made and donated a wonderful gown for the Susan G. Komen Foundation, and I was lucky enough to model it. It felt so good on and I will never forget how special I felt on stage. I loved the dress so much that I ended up bidding on it—and winning! I have worn that gown so many times. I have worn that gown to the opera ball and so many other black-tie affairs. It is timeless.

Being around Lily is a love affair in itself. Her passion is to make women look beautiful. She is very feminine; she loves creating beautiful designs that make a woman feel like a Queen for the day!

She designed a spectacular gown for an opera ball I chaired that paid tribute to the opera—that year it was Aida. That was an extraordinary night. The gown is a museum piece! Lily put her heart and soul into that gown. I could feel it. She loves to work with color and that is such a special thing to do—she celebrates colors.

Before she begins, she talks to you about the event the gown is for, and she listens carefully about how you want to feel and what the event means to you. She is a very deep thinker and contemplates how to create the perfect piece for each woman.

They broke the mold with Lily. It is near-impossible to find anyone as talented as her. She is definitely one of a kind. If my son ever gets married, I'm going to beg her to come out of retirement and design something very special for me. I feel so fortunate to have her in my life.

—Mary Poland

Mary Poland wearing a Lily Samii gown, attending the San Francisco Opera Opening Night Gala, September 2010

PATTERN	6	SEQUIN 2½ yd.
→DUCHESS←	8	Duchess 2½ yd
② C.F. TOP 1ST LAYER ×14.	10	Taffeta 5 yd
② C.B. TOP 1ST LAYER ×14.	12	Buckram 3yd
① C.F. WAISTBAND ×14.	14	Lining 2¾ yd
① C.B. WAISTBAND ×14.	16	
① C.F. SKIRT 1ST LAYER ×14.	18	Cut time: 8hrs.
① C.B. SKIRT 1ST LAYER ×14.	20	
① C.F. SKIRT 4TH LAYER ×14.		
① C.B. SKIRT 4TH LAYER ×14.		
① C.F. SKIRT 7TH LAYER ×14.		
① C.B. SKIRT 7TH LAYER ×14.		
→ORGANZA←		
① C.F. TOP 2ND LAYER		
② C.F. TOP 3RD LAYER		
② C.B. TOP 3RD LAYER		
① C.F. SKIRT 1ST LAYER ×14.		
① C.B. SKIRT 1ST LAYER ×14.		
① C.F. SKIRT 2ND LAYER ×14.		
① C.B. SKIRT 2ND LAYER ×14.		
① C.F. SKIRT 3RD LAYER ×14.		
① C.F. SKIRT 3RD LAYER		
① C.B. SKIRT 3RD LAYER ×14.		
① C.B. SKIRT 3RD LAYER		
① C.F. SKIRT 4TH LAYER ×14.		
① C.B. SKIRT 4TH LAYER ×14.		
① C.F. SKIRT 5TH LAYER ×14.		
① C.B. SKIRT 5TH LAYER ×14.		
① C.F. SKIRT 6TH LAYER ×14.		
① C.F. SKIRT 6TH LAYER		
① C.B. SKIRT 6TH LAYER ×14.		
① C.B. SKIRT 6TH LAYER		
① C.F. SKIRT 7TH LAYER ×14.		
① C.B. SKIRT 7TH LAYER ×14.		
① C.F. SKIRT 8TH LAYER ×14.	10	
① C.F. SKIRT 8TH LAYER ×14.	12	
① C.B. SKIRT 9TH LAYER ×14.	14	
① C.F. SKIRT 9TH LAYER ×14.	16	
① C.F. SKIRT 9TH LAYER	18	
① C.B. SKIRT 9TH LAYER ×14.	20	
① C.B. SKIRT 9TH LAYER		
→LACE (SEQUIN)←		REMARKS
① C.F. TOP 2ND LAYER		
① C.F. SKIRT 2ND LAYER		
① C.F. SKIRT 5TH LAYER		
① C.F. SKIRT 8TH LAYER		
① C.B. SKIRT 2ND LAYER		
① C.B. SKIRT 5TH LAYER		
① C.B. SKIRT 8TH LAYER		
→LINING←		
① C.F. TOP LINING		
① R.S.F. TOP LINING		
① L.S.F. TOP LINING		
① C.B. TOP LINING		
① C.F. SKIRT LINING		
① R.C.B. SKIRT LINING		
① L.C.B. SKIRT LINING		
① C.F. WAISTBAND		
① C.B. WAISTBAND		
→COTTON←		
① C.F. SKIRT		
① R.C.B. SKIRT		
① L.C.B. SKIRT		
① C.F. TOP 2ND LAYER		

Alison Hall Mauzé, alongside her husband Michael, wearing a Lily Samii gown at the San Francisco Ballet Opening Night Gala, 2013

Lily Samii designs are breathtakingly beautiful. I love all of her work—gowns, dresses, suits, coats, and accessories. She creates ensembles for all aspects of life. Her gowns are magical to me! They flow, rustle, shimmy, and make me feel confident and pretty. Crafted with the richest fabrics and designed to flatter, each one is a work of art. Lily's warm, kind personality, blended with her extraordinary gift for design, made it a joy to be dressed by her, and she led the way in giving back to the community. Lily is an inspiration and her designs a true gift!

—Alison Hall Mauzé

Alison pictured with her husband Michael Mauzé, wearing a Lily Samii gown to the San Francisco Ballet Opening Night Gala, 2004

From the Private Haute Couture Collection of Lily Samii

Karen Caldwell, surrounded by members of the press, wearing a Lily Samii gown at the San Francisco Opera Opening Night Gala, 2009

HER LEGACY

Just as her hometown of Isfahan, Iran, has The Eight Heavens, Lily Samii has eight core values by which she has lived her life. It is these unwavering traits that were the foundations and steps she took to reach her greatness and establish her incredible reputation in the fashion industry.

Lily Samii, San Francisco Opera Ball, 2017

INTEGRITY & HONESTY

Even as a child, Lily would speak her mind with the steadiness of an archer shooting an arrow. It is this clarity of focus that allowed her clients to open up and share their deepest desires for the gowns and outfits she would personally create for each person. If a client said she wanted a specific style and fabric, but Lily knew that cut and texture would not exemplify that person's beauty, Lily would say so and give her professional and insightful suggestions. Of course, Lily was right, and her clients always looked stunning in the gowns she designed.

INNOVATION & SKILLFULNESS

During Lily's childhood, she was always fascinated by the construction of things. That curiosity is what drove her to create clothes that fit her clients perfectly. Every angle, movement, or seam was carefully designed to give her client the feeling of wearing a jeweled gown that was as light as a feather. Lily's determination for perfection led her to new and innovative ways to create structure and movement in her gowns. Her clients were very thankful for her skillfulness because no longer did they worry about pulling up their strapless gown every ten minutes or tripping over their hem. Each detail of the gown was carefully thought through by Lily.

3 GENEROSITY & TEAMWORK

Lily respected the importance of cooperation and teamwork. She knew that as creative and innovative as she was on her own, it would take a solid team to truly transform her ideas into the empire she envisioned. And that is what she did. She compiled an incredible crew of individuals who believed in the Lily Samii dream. From sales and marketing to seamstresses and fitters, Lily found the best people and treated them with the same dignity and respect she treated royalty. Working for Lily Samii was a badge of honor, and she inspired her team to be the best they could be.

4 AUTHENTICITY & INSIGHTFULNESS

It was not just Lily's creativity that propelled her to the top of the fashion world, it was also her uncanny ability to ask her clients the right questions. Lily's queries did not revolve around the color of the gown, but instead were filled with emotion and expectation: "How do you want to feel in the dress?" "What type of occasion is this: celebration, serious, family, international, gala?" "Who will be with you when you wear this dress?" Lily's questions allowed her clients to reveal their true selves along with the emotions they wanted to feel when they wore her creations. Some needed outfits to meet kings and queens; others wanted suits to be sworn into public office; some wanted wedding gowns; and even more wanted mother-of-the-bride and groom attire. For each, there was a different mood that needed to be portrayed, and Lily was able to capture that.

QUALITY & TALENT

After the tragedy of 9/11—and the economic downturn that followed—many businesses across the country suffered huge losses. Jacobson's, one of our best accounts (they had stores from Florida to Michigan), had to close their doors after 150 years.

We tried to stay with it as much as we could, but at the end of the day wholesale had lost its novelty for me. I was repeatedly told if I could do the same design but use lower-grade fabrics to bring the cost down, they could sell it in more of their stores. I knew the value of my work and was not going to compromise. For me, changing my signature silk lining to a polyester lining was so insulting. I was too connected to my craft to lose its integrity for meager monetary gain. I decided to keep a few of our wholesale accounts and concentrate on the couture part of the business.

Every garment that left our production site has the MADE IN AMERICA label —and not only made in the USA, but in San Francisco! It wasn't always easy to maintain this level of devotion and respect to my designs, but I fought hard and sacrificed so much to be able to stay the course and, with my heart full of gratitude and honor, I can say it was all worth it!

ORIGINALITY & BEAUTY

As a designer, Lily pushed the envelope on the bold use of vibrant colors and textures in gowns. While more conservative designers stuck to traditional combinations, Lily's creativity blossomed into a kaleidoscope of patterns, silhouettes, and colors. Fuchsia and purple, chartreuse and orange—Lily's combinations were artistic expressions that moved with the grace of the fortunate ladies who wore her gowns. It was not just colors Lily played with, but also different fabrics and textures in amazingly gorgeous designs that broke all conventional rules of fashion wisdom.

LOYALTY & HUMILITY

One of the main reasons that Lily's powerful A-list of international clients were loyal to her for fifty years was because of her timeless discretion, unwavering humility, and modesty about her work. Lily is not one to grandstand or boast about her work. She is a gentle soul who takes pride in her creations with a light measure of restraint. Of course, her signature colors, textures, and trims are famous, so while she might have kept quiet about her gowns, the gowns themselves announced to the world that they were the creation of Lily Samii.

STRENGTH & FORTITUDE

Lily's life was riddled with tragic moments. From the awful fall that left her bed-ridden with broken vertebrae in her neck, to the sudden death of her young husband, Lily continued to rise up. Self-pity is not an option for her. Regardless of the misfortune, she has found her inner strength and fortitude with the conviction to continue to move forward. While others would have silently dismantled their dreams and accepted failure, Lily has found a way through every tumultuous situation that life has thrown at her.

"

My career, in its span of nearly fifty years, has been nothing short of living a dream! Hard work, determination, and good fortune of being in the right place at the right time has given me a playbook that I want to read over and over to not ever forget any nuance of it. I dedicate this book to the younger version of myself and to the many dreamers out there.

I have lived my dream for the last five decades. Besides my good fortune of having the trust of thousands of women who allowed me to be part of the most important events in their lives, as well as their loyalties to me, the other thing that I have treasured is the Lily Samii Internship Program.

The Lily Samii Internship Program

I felt it was my duty to share my art and expertise with young people. The truth is that sadly these bright students may never have the opportunity to work in the fashion industry as I knew it. With our internship program, interns were able to witness and follow the process of creating.

Throughout the years, hundreds of young people have walked through our doors. The joy of working with them has been invaluable. I was able to share my knowledge with them and, in return, they taught me so much. The young interns kept me current, and I was in awe of their knowledge of technology.

99

> " My staff were the fuel I needed to carry on. They inspired me, they kept me energized, and they made me see the world through their vibrant and youthful eyes. "

"The couture designer, whose masterpieces have been a fixture in San Francisco's high society for half a century, IS RETIRING."

This page: Lily in her downtown San Francisco office. Photo by Liz Hafalia/*San Francisco Chronicle*/Polaris

Opposite page: Mallory Moench, *San Francisco Chronicle*, Sunday, September 8, 2019

PHOTO CREDITS

Drew Altizer: pp. 217, 218, 334, 336, 339, 344, 347, 351, 363

Chris Conroy: p. 151 (bottom left, bottom right)

Peter Da Silva: pp. 247, 248

Nathan Dehart: pp. 153-57, 162-64, 221, 223-25, 227, 228, 272, 273, 278, 279, 341

Everett Collection Inc / Alamy: p. 59

Eric Klaus Fischer: pp. 141-45, 150 (left)

Laura Flippen: p. 229

Allan Grant—The Life Picture Collection: p. 61

Sasha Gulish: p. 133

Liz Hafalia: p. 373

Jack Hutcheson: p. 151 (bottom middle)

https://commons.wikimedia.org/wiki/User:Ahura21: p. 17

https://stock.adobe.com/nz/images/sheikh-lotfollah-mosque-is-one-of-the-architectural-masterpieces-of
   -iranian-architecture-that-was-built-during-the-safavid-empire-property-release-is-not-needed-for-this
   -public-place/208920091?prev_url=detail: p. 36

Moanalani Jeffrey: p. 125

Mimi Jeonj (illustration): pp. 166, 329, 333

Joe Kohen / Wire Image: pp. 214, 215

Flore Martin (illustration): p. 3

Terrence McCarthy: p. 8

Jock McDonald: pp. 170-74, 176, 177, 257, 263, 264, 266-68, 270, 271, 274-77, 280-82, 285-89, 292, 295, 296, 299,
   300, 302, 303, 305-7, 309, 310, 313, 315, 319, 320, 322, 323, 335, 342, 345, 349, 352, 355, 356

Doug Menuez: p. 131

David Paul Morris / SF Chronicle / Polaris: p. 207

Arun Nevader: pp. 233-45, 250, 251, 269

From Jennifer Newsom's Personal Archive: p. 205

Charlie Nucci: pp. 2, 179-83, 185, 186, 188-91, 193-95, 197-203, 246, 249, 253, 255, 256, 259-61

David Perez: pp. 151 (top row), 187

Ken Probst: p. 120

Lily Samii Archive: pp. 5, 15, 19, 20, 22, 23, 25, 26, 29-31, 33-35, 38-40, 42, 43, 46-49, 51-55, 62, 63, 65, 68, 73, 74, 78, 81, 85-89, 96, 97, 101, 104-9, 113-18, 123, 126, 128, 129, 134, 136-39, 158-61, 206, 208-13, 216, 230, 231, 252, 290, 291, 316, 317, 324, 325, 353, 357-61, 368, 369

Jenni Sandmark: pp. 111, 327, 328, 331, 332, 343

Sophie Spinelle: p. 150

Raymond Tom: pp. 91, 93, 94

LIFE WITHOUT PASSION

IS LIKE LOOKING AT THE WORLD

THROUGH A GRAY LENS.

LIFE WITH PASSION, HOWEVER,

IS LIKE LOOKING AT THE WORLD

THROUGH A KALEIDOSCOPE.

—**LILY SAMII**